THE PIONEERS

OF

BUDDHIST REVIVAL IN INDIA

Bibliotheca Indo-Buddhica No. 70

The Pioneers of Buddhist Revival in India

D. C. AHIR

SRI SATGURU PUBLICATIONS
A Division of
Indian Books Centre
Delhi—India

Published by :
SRI SATGURU PUBLICATIONS
Indological and Oriental Publishers
a Division of :
INDIAN BOOKS CENTRE,
40/5, Shakti Nagar,
Delhi-110007
INDIA

I.S.B,N—81-7030-212-9

Printed at :
A. R. Printers, D-102 New Seelampur,
Delhi-110053.

PREFACE

The rediscovery of Buddhism in India began in 1891 with the founding of the Maha Bodhi Society of India by Anagarika Dharmapala, and reached its climax in 1956 when Dr. Ambedkar gave a clarion call to his followers to seek refuge in the Buddha-Dhamma. Presented here are short biographies of 30 Pioneer Buddhists, from Anagarika to Ambedkar, who devoted their lives to the cause of Buddhism, and made it once again a living religion in India.

Having been associated with the Buddhist movement since 1952, I had the good fortune of personally knowing as many as 12 out of 30 Pioneers, whose biographies are included in this book. They being : Devapriya Valisinha, Venerable N. Jinaratana, Ven. U. Dhammaratana, Ven. M. Sangharatana, Ven. Dharmarakshita, Ven, L. Ariyawansa (all of the Maha Bodhi Society of which I am a Life Member), Mahapandit Rahul Sankrityayan, Bhadant Anand Kausalyayan, Ven. Jagdish Kashyap, Ven. Kushak Bakula, Dr. R.L. Soni and Dr. B.R. Ambedkar. Therefore, much of what I write here is based on my personal knowledge and observation. Care has, however, been taken to consult all the sources that are available today in order to present an authentic and accurate account of the contribution of each pioneer in the revival movement. I record my thanks to all the listed sources which enabled me to present this treatise, the first of its kind, on the lives of the Pioneers of Buddhist Revival in India.

17 September 1989 D.C. AHIR

CONTENTS

THE BLESSED NAME

Bring to this country once again
the blessed name
Which made the land of thy birth sacred
to all distant lands !
Let Thy great awakening under the bodhi tree
be fulfilled.
Sweeping away the evil of unreason
and let, at the end of an oblivious night,
freshly blossom out in India
Thy remembrance !
Bring life to the mind that is inert,
thou Illimitable Light and life !
Let the air become vital with
Thy inspiration !
Let open the doors that barred,
and the resounding conch shell
proclaim Thy arrival at Bharat's gate.
Let, through innumerable voices,
the gospel of an immeasurable love
announce Thy call.

Rabindranath Tagore

INTRODUCTION

Buddhism dominated the Indian scene for about 1000 years from BC 3rd century to AD 7th century. Then it began to decline for the reasons which were external as well as internal. By the end of the 12th century AD, Buddhism in India had been completely engulfed by the dark clouds. And in the following centuries, thousands of Buddhist shrines were either destroyed, plundered or usurped by its opponents. When the monks were no more; monasteries had been destroyed or deserted; the Buddhist scriptures and other literature also perished; leaving nc trace whatsoever of the great religion of the Buddha.

After a long spell of darkness, light dawned on Buddhism in India when the British Civil Servants started bringing to light its treasures hidden under dust and debris. Asokan Pillars standing in the open were the first to be noticed by the curious foreigners. The romantic story of the archaeological discoveries began in 1750 with the discovery of some fragments of an Asokan inscription on the Delhi-Meerut Pillar which now stands on the Ridge, Delhi. In the same year, the Allahabad—Kosam (Kausambi) Pillar at Allahabad was discovered. This was followed by the discovery of the Lauriya—Araraj (Radhia) Pillar in 1784 and the Barabara Hill Cave inscription in 1785. In 1785 again, the Delhi-Topra Pillar at Ferozshah Kotla, Delhi was discovered by Captain Polier. He presented some drawings of its inscription to Sir William Jones who had founded in Calcutta in 1784 the Asiatic Society of Bengal to collect, decipher and interpret the archaeological and other specimens discovered by its members.

By 1836, a number of Rock and Pillar inscriptions had been discovered in various parts of India. But no body knew either their contents or the name of their creator. No Indian scholar was competent enough to decipher the most ancient inscriptions of India which were found not only on the rocks and pillars but on the coins as well. In 1837, James Prinsep, a high official of the Indian Mint and Secretary of the Asiatic Society of Bengal, succeeded, after several years of assiduous study and hard work, in deciphering the inscriptions which were written in Prakrit. In July 1837, he published fascimiles, phonetic transcriptions and English translation of the seven pillar Edicts, the opening words of which were: 'Thus spake the beloved of gods, King Piyadasi.' Who was King Piyadasi still remained a mystery. Luckily, in the same year, George Turnour translated and published in English the Mahavamsa, a Pali chronicle of Sri Lanka. The occurrence of the word 'Piyadasi' in the Mahavamsa helped Prinsep in identifying King Piyadasi as the great Buddhist Emperor Asoka. In 1838, James Prinsep deciphered and published translation of the Girnar Rock inscription in Gujarat (discovered in 1822) and the Dhauli Rock inscription in Orissa (discovered in 1837). Thus, James Prinsep, working almost single-handed, made available just within a period of ten months, a major portion of the Asokan inscriptions.

The deciphering of the Asokan lipi and the identification of Asoka was an epoch-making event. It enriched the history of India and of Buddhism to such an extent that all history books had to be re-written.

The advent of Alexander Cunningham (1814-1893) accelerated the discovery and restoration of the archaeological sites in India. He was undoubtedly the greatest archaeologist and hero of the Buddhist renaissance period. Cunningham was born in England on 23 January 1814. After completing his education, he arrived in India in 1833 and joined the Bengal Engineers as 2nd Lieutenant. Between 1836—40, he served as A.D.C. to the Governor General of India, Lord Auckland. In 1837, he excavated Sarnath at his own expense and made drawings of the objects discovered by him. In 1851, while employed as an engineer in Gwalior State, Cunningham opened the mighty stupas of Sanchi and discovered the sacred relics of the two chief disciples of Lord Buddha, namely, Sariputta and Moggallana from inside the Stupa 3. A detailed account of his findings at Sanchi and other Buddhist sites around Sanchi was published by him in 1854 in a book titled "The Bhilsa Topes or Buddhist Monuments of Central India". For two years (1856-58) Cunningham was Chief Engineer in Burma. By 1861, Cunningham had risen to the rank of Major General. In that year, he was appointed as the first Archaeological Surveyor of India in the newly created archaeological department of northern India. In 1871 Cunningham became the first Director General of Archaeological Survey of India.

Cunningham's zeal and interest in the archaeological matters opened a new vista in the study of ancient monuments. As luck would have it, a French scholar, M. Stanisla Julien, had in the meanwhile published a translation of the travel accounts of Hiuen Tsang, the famous Chinese pilgrim, who was in India from AD 629-644. Following the footsteps of Hiuen Tsang, Cunningham went round; visited all the sites described by the Chinese pilgrim; and with the greatest preservering labour and enterprise succeeded in identifying most of the Buddhist shrines. In his monumental work 'Ancient Geography of India, Part I, the Buddhist Period, 'Cunningham recapitulated the glorious history of the Buddhist remains and monuments scattered all over the country. In 1870, he excavated the vicinity of the Maha Bodhi Temple, and discovered Vajrasana, the most sacred place sitting where the Buddha had attained Supreme Enlightenment. Later, he published his conclusions in the volume titled "Maha Bodhi or the Great Buddhist Temple at Buddha Gaya." In 1873-74, Cunningham excavated the Stupa of Bharhut and rescued the finest Buddhist art from further oblivion. His publication 'Stupa of Bharhut' which came out in 1879, throws a flood of light on this most ancient Buddhist shrine in Central India. The Asokan inscriptions also received Cunningham's proper attention as it was he who in 1877 published all the then known inscriptions in one volume. During the period he worked as Director General of Archaeological Survey (1871—1885), Cunningham also published 24 volumes as 'Reports of the Archaeological Survey of India'. Of these, half the reports were written by Cunningham himself, and the rest by his assistants, J.D. Beglar and A.C.L. Carlleyle, under his supervision and guidance. All his writings have the stamp of scholarship and are replete with facts and figures based on actual research on site.

Sir Alexander Cunningham retired from service in September 1885 and returned to London, after fifty years in India. During his retirement in London, until his death on 28 November 1893, he worked on the mass of material he had collected and wrote several books on Buddhism. Cunningham was a remarkable man in all respects, and India was fortunate in having attracted him. Buddhists in particular owe him a special debt.

Cunningham was succeeded by James Burgess as Director General of Archaeological Survey of India. Burgess, who had been working since 1874 as Archaeological Surveyor of western and southern India, made a comprehensive survey of the Buddhist caves and published his findings in 1883 in his well-known book "Buddhist Cave Temples and their Inscriptions".

Dr. Bhagwanlal Indraji was the first Indian archaeologist He discovered in 1882 fragments of an Asokan Rock Edict as well as a Stupa at Sopara near Bombay. The most remarkable discovery by him at Sopara was that of the five relic-caskets from the Stupa datable to about AD 160.

A further fillip to the renaissance of Buddhism was given by the literary activities of the Western scholars. The pioneer Indian scholar was Rajendra Lal Mitra (1824-1891). His works, particularly, 'Buddha Gaya'. The Hermitage of the Sakya Sage' (1877), Sanskrit Buddhist Literature of Nepal (1882) and Lalitavistara (1887) aroused considerable interest in Buddhist studies.

The researches of all these explorers, archaeologists and scholars were helpful in creating a new awakening amongst the people but no body had as yet thought seriously of the Buddhist revival in India. This happened only in 1891 with the arrival of Anagarika Dharmapala, a young Sinhala Buddhist.

The year 1891 is the most memorable year in the history of Indian Buddhism. It was in 1891 that Anagarika Dharmpala initiated the Buddhist revival movement in India. It was in 1891 again that Dr. B R. Ambedkar, who was to change later the course of the history of Buddhism, was born. Equally memorable is the year 1956; the year of the 2,500th Buddha Jayanti Celebrations. It was in 1956 that the revival movement reached its climax when Dr. Ambedkar, and his half a million followers, embraced Buddhism at a historic conversion ceremony at Nagpur on 14 October. Hence, this study is confined to those pioneers who either flourished or adopted the Buddhist way of life during the period from 1891 to 1956, and marched ahead of others carrying aloft the banner of Dhamma.

At the head of the convoy of the Pioneers of Buddhist Revival in India is Anagarika Dharmapala, a great son of Sri Lanka, who was the first to hoist the flag of Buddhism in modern India. Inspired by his missionary zeal, many more sons of Sri Lanka also devoted their lives to the cause of Buddhism in India. Of them, six prominent ones are included here. Two missionary monks from Burma and Japan also made significant contribution to the revival movement.

The Buddhist revival movement gained momentum when some sons of the soil donned the yellow robes, and devoted their lives to the propagation of Buddhism. Of the eleven Pioneer Indian Buddhist monks, eight came from the Hindu families. They were; Mahavira (1890), Dharmananda Kosambi (1902), Bodhananda (1914), Anand Kausalyayan (1928), Rahul Sankrityayan (1930), Jagdish Kashyap (1934), Nandabansha (1937) and Dharmarakshita (1942). The prominent monks who came from the traditional Buddhist families were ; Kripasaran, L. Ariyawansa (both from Chittagong), and Kushak Bakula (from Ladakh). Their efforts were supplemented by some lay Buddhist leaders. Of them, nine have been included here. The last and the greatest pioneer of Buddhist revival in India was Dr. Ambedkar. Like a Bodhisattva, he employed 'skillful means' to bring a large mass of humanity to the fold of Buddhism.

For facility of presentation, the biographies have been divided into three groups. In the first group are all the nine foreign missionaries. They are followed by Indian Buddhist monks, and the lay Buddhists come last. Though the selection is confined upto the year 1956, the biographies are, however, uptodate. As such, the story of the Buddhist revival presented here covers nearly 100 years from 1891 onward. The Epilogue sums up the contribution of the Pioneers of Buddhist Revival in India from Anagarika to Ambedkar.

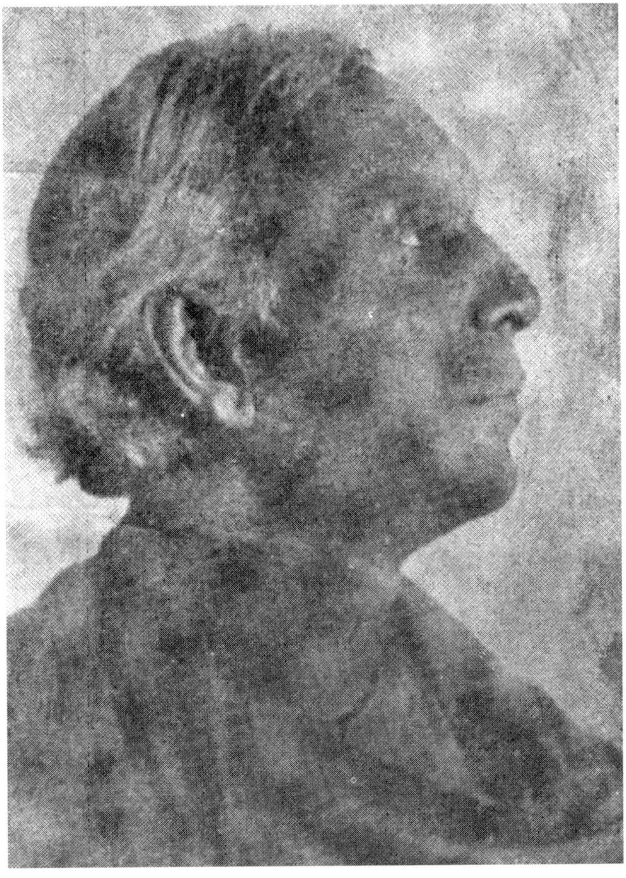

Anagarika Dharmapala

1864—1933

1

ANAGARIKA DHARMAPALA

Anagarika Dharmapala, the founder of the Maha Bodhi Society and initiater of the Buddhist revival movement in India, was born on 17 September 1864 in a Buddhist family of Ceylon (Sri Lanka). His father, Don Carolis Mudaliar Hewavitarne was having a furniture manufacturing business in Colombo. His mother, Mallika, was the daughter of another businessman of Colombo, who had established the first Buddhist monastic college in Ceylon, the Vidyodaya Pirivena at Colombo. By the time of his birth, the national religion and culture of Ceylon had fallen to the lowest pitch of degeneration as 'successive waves of Portaguese, Dutch and British invasions had swept away much of the traditional culture of the country, and the Sinhalese were taught to be ashamed of their religion, their culture, their language, their race and their colour.' Not only that, the Buddhists were even compelled to declare themselves as Christians. And children born of Buddhist parents had to be taken for registration to a Chruch, where some biblical name would be bestowed on them. Following this practice, the first child of Don Carolis Mallika was named 'Don David'. However, he was brought up by his devout Buddhist parents in the traditional Sinhalese culture. His pious mother, in particular, instilled in him the traditional Buddhist piety which had been the heritage of the Sinhalese race for more than 2000 years. He got further grounding in the Buddha-Dhamma as a child when he was sent, at the age of eight, to a Sinhala private school and learnt his lessons there for two years from a venerable monk well conversant with the Sinhala tradition and literature.

David Hewavitarne, or Dharmapala as he was later known, had the first taste of the aggressively missionary atmosphere at an anglican (C.M.S.) School at Kotte near Colombo. Here he was daily forced to attend service in the Church at 6.30 A.M., and in the class he had to recite some verses from Genesis or Mathew. But the attitude of the Christian missionaries to Buddhist scriptures was quite repulsive. One Sunday, when Dharmapala was quietly reading a pamphlet on the Four Noble Truths, the boarding master came upto him; snatched the pamphlet and threw it out of the room. Soon after this incident, Dharmapala left this school and joined in September 1878 St. Thomas Collegiate School in North Colombo, where the children of the elite received their schooling. Here his uncompromising championship of his ancestral faith, Buddha-Dhamma, brought him into conflict with the rigid discipline of the school. On the eve of the Wesak (Buddha Jayanti), he approached the head of the institution, and after explaining how this day was the 'Thrice Sacred Day' for the Buddhists, sought permission to spend the day at home in worship and religious observances. The headmaster refused permission saying that 'he did not feel justified in granting a holiday merely for the observance of a Buddhist festival'. Hearing this, Dharmapala picked up his books and walked out of the school for the day. Next day, he was not only reprimanded for his insubordination but was also punished with cane-strokes on the seat of his trousers. As in the following two years also, his request for the observance of Buddha Jayanti at home was not granted, he absented himself from the school, and was given usual punishment for the same. This experience made him resolve to work for the revival of Buddhism. His resolve was further strengthened after listening to the forceful lectures on Buddhism by the Venerable Bhikkhu Migetuvatte Gunananda, the greatest orator and debator of Sri Lanka at that time, and incumbent of the Kotahena Vihara, which was on his way to St. Thomas College. Dharmapala was not only a frequent visitor to this Temple but had also become a favourite of the Venerable monk, who had challenged the Christian missionaries and humbled them in a public debate held at Panadure near Colombo in 1873.

A turning point in the life of Dharmapala was the arrival of Colonel Henry Steele Olcott, an American, and Madame Helena Petrovna Blavatsky, a Russian lady, in Colombo in May 1880. They had jointly founded the Theosophical Society at New York in 1875, and were much impressed by the triumph of Venerable Gunanada over his Christian adversaries in a public debate in 1873. Dharmapala had been earlier given by Ven. Gunananda a copy of the first issue of 'The Theosophist', edited by Col. Olcott, and had liked it. On coming to know of their arrival, he became excited. On 21 May 1880, Col. Olcott and Madame Blavatsky publicly embraced Buddhism at Galle, South Ceylon, by taking the Three Refuges and Five Precepts in Pali in the presence of thousands of Buddhists from the surrounding villages. Dharmapala was also present along with his father and uncle. He was very much impressed by the demeanour of the visiting pair. Later, when in June Col. Olcott delivered his first lecture on Buddhism in Colombo, Dharmapala met him and Madame Blavatsky there after the meeting. From that day, he felt drawn to them.

When the Buddhist renaissance movement began to gain momentum in Ceylon., the Christians became restless. And in March 1883 a Catholic mob brutally assaulted a Buddhist procession on its way to Migettuvatta Gunananda's temple in Kotahena. This infuriated Dharmapala's father, and he refused to allow him to study any longer in a Christian School, even though he had not yet matriculated. In 1884, Dharmapala joined the Theosophical Society, alongwith two other monks. They were initiated personally by Col. Olcott and Madame Blavatsky, and became life members of the Society. Soon thereafter, Dharmapala accompanied Madame Blavatsky to Adyar, Madras, the headquarters of the Theosophical Society, and stayed there for sometime. On return to Ceylon, Dharmapala thought of working fulltime for the Buddhist cause in co-operation with the Theosophical Society, and sought his parent's permission to leave home and to take Brahmacharya vows in order to dedicate his life to the service of the Dhamma. While his father agreed to his request reluctantly, his mother gave her blessings willingly. Accordingly, he became an Anagarika or 'Homeless' and started living and working at the Theosophical Society's office in Colombo.

In February 1886, Col. Olcott and Rev. C.W. Leadbeater arrived in Colombo with the idea of collecting money for the Buddhist Educational Fund. They had planned to tour the whole Island, and needed the services of a Sinhala interpreter. In the meanwhile, Dharmapala had taken up the job of a junior clerk in the Ceylon Education Department. On knowing their plans, Dharmapala promptly offered his services and agreed to accompany them; and applied for long leave with the intention of resigning ultimately. For the next two months, the 'trio' traversed every nook and corner of the country in a two-storeyed cart; Col. Olcott highlighting the good points in Buddhism, and Dharmapala translating the same in the simple Sinhalese language for the consumption of the village folk. This preaching tour proved a very valuable experience for young Dharmapala; it widened his vision and made him more deterimined to work for the revival and regeneration of the national faith which was crumbling as a result of the hostile Christian missionaries and their hirelings.

On return to Colombo, Dharmapala resigned from the post of junior clerk in the Education Department and became a full-time activist in the Buddhist revival movement. From 1885 to 1889, he devoted himself to the affairs to the Theosophical Society and Buddhism which prepared him for the great missionary work in the coming years. During this period, Dharmapala and Col. Olcott established a printing press; started bringing out the first Buddhist weekly in Sinhalese, Sandaresa: and later in December 1888 founded its counterpart in English 'The Buddhist' under the editorship of Rev. Leadbeater. While intensively engaged in this Dhamma work, Don David assumed the name of Dharmapala or 'Defender of the Faith'. Being homeless, he subsequently came to be known as Anagarika Dharmapala.

On an invitation from the Buddhists of Japan, Col. Olcott went to Japan in January 1889 to attend the Buddhist Convention at Kyoto. Dharmapala also accompanied him. Though he fell ill immediately on arrival in Japan, and had to be hospitalised, yet Dharmapala came back more determined to carry on the revival work after having seen the devotion and dedication of the Japanese people to the Buddha-Dhamma. Then came another turning point in the life of Dharmapala. Sir Edwin Arnold, the world famous author of the 'Light of Asia' had visited Buddha Gaya in 1885, and later written a series of articles in the London Weekly 'Telegraph' of which he was the editor. He drew attention of the Buddhists to the deplorable condition of the Maha Bodhi Temple, and urged them to save it from further desecration. Having read that, Dharmapala decided to visit the holy Buddhist shrines in India in order to see for himself the condition thereof.

On 18 January 1891, Dharmapala, accompanied by a Japanese monk, Kozen Gunaratana, arrived in Banaras, and on 20 January,

Babu Upendranath Basu drove them over to Sarnath. Dharmapala was shocked to see the horrible condition of the sacred site where Lord Buddha had preached His First Sermon and turned the Wheel of Law. The holy site was now completely in ruins, deserted, and haunt of the pigs. He sighed and wrote in his diary "What a pity, no Buddhists are occupying the place to preserve them (the stupa and carvings) from the hand of the vandals". At Bodh Gaya, where they reached on January 22, Dharmapala was visibly moved as under the Mahants's charge the Maha Bodhi Temple was being shamefully neglected and desecrated. To quote his own words :

"After taking breakfast, I went in the company of [1]Durga Bubu and Dr.[2] Chatterjee to Buddha Gaya-the most sacred spot to the Buddhists. After driving 6 miles (from Gaya) we arrived at the holy spot. Within a mile you could see lying scattered here and there broken statues etc., of our blessed Lord. At the entrance to the Mahant's temple on both sides of the portico there are statues of our Lord in the attitude of meditation and expounding the Law. How elevating ! The sacred Vihara-the Lord sitting on his throne and the great solemnity which pervades all round makes the heart of the pious devotee weep. How delightful. ! As soon as I touched with my forehead the Vajrasana a sudden impulse came to my mind. It prompted me to stop here and take care of this sacred spot-so sacred that nothing in the world is equal to this place where Prince Sakyasinha gained Enlightenment under the Bodhi Tree. When the sudden impulse came to me, I asked Kozen priest whether he would join me, and he joyously assented and more than this he had been thinking the same thing. We both solemnly promised that we would stop here until some Buddhist priests came to take charge of the place".

Having resolved to regain the control of the Maha Bodhi Temple from the Saivite Mahant, whose ancestors had occupied it around the close of the 16th century, Dharmapala decided to stay put at Bodh Gaya till some satisfactory arrangements were made to preserve the sanctity of the sacred shrine. So he moved to the nearby Burmese Rest House; built in 1875 by King Mindon of

1. Durga Sankar Bhattacharya.
2. Dr. Hari Das Chatterjee.

Burma, and as soon as he had settled there he started writing letters to scores of people in Ceylon, Burma and India describing the pitiable condition of the holiest of the holy Buddhist shrine. And pleading for their co-operation, help and assistance for the re-establishment of the Sangha there. He also wrote long articles for the same purpose in Sinhalese and English respectively in the 'Sandaresa' and 'The Buddhist' published from Colombo. In the meanwhile, Dharmapala also made enquiries from the officials about the ownership of the Temple. When the Collector of Gaya, informed him that the Temple together with its revenues, belonged to the Mahant, adding that with the help of the Government it might be possible for the Buddhists to buy it from him, Dharmapala immediately started planning collection of the required funds and left for Burma via Calcutta. After arousing interest of the Burmese Buddhists in the restoration of the Maha Bodhi Temple and having received promises for financial assistance, Dharmapala returned to Colombo in May 1891. And on May 31 there, he founded the 'The Buddha Gaya Maha Bodhi Society' to work for "the establishment of a Buddhist Monastery and founding a Buddhist College, and maintaining a staff of Buddhist Bhikkhus at Buddha Gaya".

Ven. Hikkaduwe Sumangala Maha Nayaka Thera, Principal of the Vidyodaya Pirivena, Colombo, was the first President of the Maha Bodhi Society and Dharmapala was its first General Secretary.

After forming the Society, Dharmapala thought of establishing the Bhikkhu Sangha at Buddha Gaya on the Full Moon Day of the month of Asadha, the Day on which Lord Buddha had preached His First Sermon at Sarnath. With this object in view, he appealed to the Bhikkhus of Ceylon, and succeeded in obtaining four monks : Dunuwila Chandjoti, Matale Sumangala, Anuradhapura Pemananda and Galle Sudassana. Accompanied by them, he reached Buddha Gaya on the eve of the Asadha Full Moon Day, and reverently hoisted the Buddhist flag under the Bodhi Tree on the morning of Asadha Poornima. Elated on seeing the Buddhist flag on the sacred spot, Dharmapala recorded in his diary as under :

"Ah, how beautifully it flutters in the moonlight breez! May the mission be success! I hope and sincerely trust that the priests may be a light to the people and will lead a life of purity, and show the people of India the intrinsic merits of our holy religion".

Having installed the four Buddhist monks in the Burmese Rest House, Dharmapala approached the Mahant for the purchase of a plot of land for the Maha Bodhi Society's office but he was greatly distressed to find the delaying tactics of the Mahant and the indifferent attitude of the Collector of Gaya. Hurt by this obstructive attitude, Dharmapala decided to organize an International Buddhist Conference at Buddha Gaya. This Conference, first of its kind on Indian soil after centuries of darkness, was held on 31 October 1891. The representatives from Sri Lanka, China, Japan and Chittagong attended this Conference and pondered over the ways and means to save the Seat of Buddha's Enlightenment from further desecration.

At the beginning of 1892, the office of the Maha Bodhi Society was shifted to Calcutta, where the home of a large hearted businessman, Neel Comul Mookerjee, became the home of Dharmapala. In May, 1892, the Anagarika founded the Maha Bodhi journal, the first of its kind in India. How this journal, which is still preaching the Dhamma in all parts of the world, was started by Dharmapala with a paltry sum of Rs. 25 has been beautifully told by St. Nihal Singh. He says :

"As the thrice blessed day of the Vaisakh Poornima in 1892 was drawing nigh a 'brain wave' struck the Anagarika Dharmapala. This was almost as mighty as had been the one that the previous year had led to the organisation of the 'Buddh-Gaya Maha Bodhi Society' as it was called when 'established at Colombo, May 31, 1891'. The wave impelled the organiser of that Society—he (then signing H. Dharmapala) modestly styled himself as its General Secretary—to embark upon the publication of a monthly organ to serve a multiplicity of purposes.

These he described to me when near the beginning of this century I was living with him for a while and assisting him with proof reading, a little writing and correspondence in the front room of the tiny cottage that he had hastily run up for himself in the shadow of the Dhamek stupa in Sarnath. The Journal would carry the news of the Society's activities to its constituents, supporters and sympathisers wherever they be. His eyes even then surveyed the globe, not merely Ceylon, India, Burma, (then integrated with India) and other Buddhist countries. Of Thibet (as usually written) Siam (now Thailand) and Japan he was in particular conscious.

It would contain articles and (what I term) articlettes relating to various phases of the Dhamma. These would be educative, rather than controversial : but nothing that animadverted against the Lord's Law or those who walked upon the Middle Path would go unchallenged in its pages".

"It is one thing to desire a publication and to know that the publication of one's heart would serve many useful purposes. It is quite another thing to have the wherewithal for starting it. Dharmapala at this stage (1892) was without any backing save the small allowance (Rs. 50 a month, I seem to remember it was) and an occasional 'hand out' from his mother, who dearly loved the first fruit of her young womb and believed in his mission in life-his striving in the interest of the sasana. He would have been hard put to it in that metropolis (so then was Calcutta) but for the hospitality extended by Neel Comul Mookerjee, both freely and cordially.

An accident occurred just when he was feeling the need of a monthly or even a quarterly organ for his recently established Society the mission of which was to take over the Asoka-built fane at Gaya and to revive Buddhism not only in the land in which the Vanquisher of this kalpa was born as all the preceding Buddhas had been, but also to revitalise the Dhamma in other countries and to propagate it in America and Europe.

In itself it was of a trivial character. It could, in fact, have been noticed only by a person who had exiled himself from a prosperous home, had thrust away from himself the prosperity that he assuredly could have built for himself and the pleasures in which he, had he so liked, could have indulged and was subsisting on a pittance from that opulent home when not enjoying hospitality extended to him through some one's kindliness of heart.

The sum of Rs. 25—a trifle even in those days except for a man like Dharmapala, had been received or was it collected from some devout Buddhist or Buddhists for a specific purpose. That purpose was to buy for a Bhikkhu passage on the deck of one of the boats that cleaved the breast of Ganga Mai (as Bengalis called the Hooghli) and of the Bay of Bengal and going up the Rangoon river made fast to the jetty at Rangoon. Once that dedicated worker got there the warm-hearted people of that city would take care of him. For one reason or another, it really does not matter what, the plan went awry. The money remained unspent.

That mighty sum burned a hole in the hyper-conscientious Dharmapala's pocket. It did not belong to him, he told himself. He could not—and would not—put it to any private use. What was he to do with it. Then the 'brain wave' struck him. 'Hullo !' he said to himself. 'Here is the opportunity for which I have been looking. The gods have vouchsafed it. With this sum I should be able to make a start with the Journal that I have been longing to bring out.'

Coming as he did from a stock that on both sides had made a success of worldly affairs, there was beneath idealism a hard core of practicality within him. This came to his rescue, even at that moment when the 'brain wave' had struck him. It sent him to a printing press to make sure about costs. The manager of the establishment was both shrewd and sympathetic. He was used to getting a coat out of cloth that others dismissed as insufficient and making the coat look nice. Advising Dharampala to cut his coat according to the cloth he had, he worked out the details. They were a magazine of 8 pages, printed in small but readable type on paper fairly substantial. The format recommended—folio 8vo (roughly 8″×11″, when trimmed) - suggested suited him, It would give him plenty of room to spread. It would look neat, too.

Delighted with the way things had worked out, he made up his mind on the spot to go ahead with the scheme. As he must have the first number out by the full-moon day that was the day of days with him and his fellow-Buddhists, he had very little time for getting the 'copy' ready. 'I will do it' he told the Manager. And he did".

The first issue of the Maha Bodhi came out, as planned, in May 1892 with its motto 'the Buddha's great exhortation to his first sixty disciples', and since then every issue begins with the same moto :

"Go Ye, O Bhikkhus and wander forth for the gain of the many, the welfare of the many, in compassion for the world, for the good, for the gain, for the welfare of Devas and men. Proclaim O Bhikkhus, the doctrine glorious, preach Ye a life of holiness, perfect and pure."

While Anagarika Dharmpala was staying in Calcutta and working with 'unflagging zeal and tireless energy' for the cause for which he had dedicated his life, hostile winds were blowing at Bodh Gaya. In January, 1893, when Col. Olcott arrived in Calcutta, they decided to visit Bodh Gaya. On their arrival at Bodh Gaya on 4 February, they found that the previous evening the Mahant's men had severely beaten up two of the monks, Bhikkhu Sumangala and another while they were peacefully engaged in reading the scriptures. Horrified by this unprovoked attack, Col. Olcott at once met the Mahant to find out the reasons for this cowardly act. Saying that he had ownership rights on the entire property at Bouh Gaya, the Mahant objected to the presence of the monks. He also refused either to sell or lease the land on any terms, or to allow the Buddhists to erect a Rest House for the pilgrims. Meanwhile, Ven. Sumangala was admitted in the hospital, and a criminal case was filed by Dharmapala against the assailants. Ven. Sumangala however, thought otherwise. From the hospital bed he sent an application to the police that neither he nor his fellow monks could be witnesses to the case and cause their assailants to be punished. On going through this application, the District Superintendent of Police is said to have remarked that 'I always thought these Indian priests made a living out of religion. These Buddhist priests from Ceylon actually practise it".

In July 1893, Dharmapala, after entrusting the journal to Sarat Chandra Das, left for America to attend the World Parliament of Religions, to be held at Chicago in September, to which he had been invited as the representative of the Theravada Buddhists. On his way to America, Dharmapala spent some time in London where he was welcomed by Sir Edwin Arnold, Rev. Leadbeater and others. He also met Rhys Davids, the great Pali scholar. At the Parliament of World Religions, the first of its kind to be held anywhere in the World, Dharmapala presented his Paper, "The World's Debt to Buddha' written in simple but forceful and lucid language, in so gracious and dignified manner that it made profound influence on the audience. "So striking was the impression made by the young preacher from Ceylon", says a report, "that whereas his colleague Vivekananda was compared with the noble but possionate Othello, Dharmapala was compared with no less a person than Jesus Christ." He gave later a series of lectures on Buddhism, and that he would lecture in the Athenaeum building on Buddhism and Theosophy was sufficient to attract an audience too large for the hall. A significant success of Dharmapala was the embracing of Buddhism by C. T. Strauss of New York, a life-long student of philosophy and comparative religion. After listening to the Anagarika's address to the World Religions Parliament, Mr. Strauss expressed his desire to become a Buddhist and then and there took refuge in the Buddha-Dhamma. He thus became the first American to become a Buddhist on American soil.

The Parliament of Religions ended on 27 September, 1893. After delivering a few more lectures in America, Dharmapala sailed for India via Japan and China. A chance meeting with Mrs. Mary Elizabeth Mikhala Foster on board the S. S. Oceanic at Honolulu on 18 October 1893 proved of immense significance both for Mrs. Foster as well as for Dharmapala. Mrs. Foster was born in the far off Hawaii islands in the Pacific Ocean and was a descendent on her mother's side of King Kamehameha the Great of Hawai. She was married to a wealthy merchant of North America. It is said that she was of an indomitable temper which she was unable to control. As a remedy for this ailment, Dharmapala advised her to cultivate will-power, and to repeat the formula "I will be good, I will control the rising anger". These simple words of a practising Buddhist worked wonders. Mrs. Foster was able to get over her temper and gained serenity. She was so deeply impressed by this change that she decided to divert her enormous wealth for the spread of the gospel of the Buddha for which Dharmapala was trying hard.

From Honolulu, Dharmapala moved further and reached Yokohama in Japan. From Japan, he came back to India by way of China Siam (Thailand), Ceylon (Sri Lanka) and reached Calcutta on 31 March 1894. On April 11, he went to Gaya with the intention of installing the beautiful Buddha image, gifted by the Japanese Buddhists, in the upper chamber of the Maha Bodhi Temple. The Collector of Gaya, however advised him 'to win over the Hindu opinion to his side' in the first instance. He accordingly went to Banaras and met the brahmin leaders. The orthodox Hindus not only opposed his proposal of installing the Buddha image in the Maha Bodhi Temple, which they claimed was a Hindu temple because Buddha was an incarnation of Vishnu, but also threatened him with dire consequences in case he tried to do so of his own. In view of this, Dharmapala postponed the installation for some time. Unmindful of these threats, however, Dharmapala decided to instal the Buddha image of his own after a few months. It was 25 February 1895. Dharmapala records in his diary :

"At 2 in the morning I woke up and sat in meditation for a little time and then my mind suggested, as it did yesterday under the Bodhi Tree, to take the Japanese Image to the Maha Bodhi Temple. I woke up the priests and then asked them to sit in contemplation for a time Then it was decided that we should take the Image early morning from Gaya to Buddha Gaya. In silence I vowed 7 times giving up my life for the Buddha's sake. Before dawn we packed the Image and by 7 were off to Buddha Gaya. Soon after our arrival at Buddha Gaya, the boxes containing the Image were taken upstairs to the Maha Bodhi Temple and when we were going to light candles, the Mahant's gosains came up and threatening me asked me to remove the Image. Oh, it was painful indeed. Buddhists are not allowed to worship in their own Temple".

Finding Dharmapala reluctant to remove the Image, the Mahant's men, who were forty-fifty in number, assaulted him and other monks, and threw the Buddha Image in the courtyard below. The Buddha Image was later kept by Dharmapala in the Burmese Rest House. The Mahant and some Hindu organisations, particularly the British India Association, London, later tried to get the Buddha Image removed even from the Rest House on the plea that "it was offensive to the Hindus". But the Government did not yield. In the meanwhile a criminal case had been filed against the Mahant's men. Finding the miscreants guilty, the Magistrate of Gaya, sentenced them to one month's simple imprisonment and a fine of one hundred rupees each. This judgement was upheld by the District Court to which the assailants had appealed. Surprisingly, however, the two judges of the Calcutta High Court sided with the orthodoxy; quashed the sentence and refunded the fines saying that 'the assailants represented the interests of the Mahant'.

The year 1896 saw the first organised celebration of the Buddha Jayanti in India after the downfall of Buddhism from the land of its birth about 700 years earlier. This was on May 26 at Calcutta, the primary centre of activities of Dharmapala ever since his arrival in India. The first ever Buddha Jayanti function in modern India was presided over by Narendra Nath Sen, the editor of 'Indian Mirror', who enthusiastically supported the revival movement. A few weeks after this, Anagarika Dharmapala sailed for America at the invitation of Dr. Paul Carus, founder of the American Buddhist Society, and after doing useful Dhamma-duta work in America, London, Paris and Rome, he returned to Ceylon towards the close of 1897. The year 1898 was spent by him in Ceylon, returning to India only in the beginning of 1899. For the past seven years Dharmapala had concentrated on the Buddha Gaya Temple case. Now he thought of doing something concrete for the revival of Buddhism. As a first step, he made an extensive lecture-tour of North India. Starting from Calcutta on 20 February 1899, he reached Lahore on 2nd March. From Lahore, he went to Rawalpindi, Peshawar, Nowshera, Mardan, Hasan Abdal and Abbottabad. From Abbatobad, he returned to Lahore via Rawalpindi, on 25 March and started his journey for Amritsar the same evening. On his way back, he visited Ludhiana, Ambala, Saharanpur, Thanesar, Kurukshetra, Karnal, Delhi, Meerut, Aligarh, Hathras, Mathura, Agra, Kanpur, Banaras, Gaya, Buddha Gaya, Bankipore and reached Calcutta on 8 May. He writes : "From 20 February to this day I have travelled; I spent nearly Rs. 200/- preached the Doctrine of Righteousness to many. Poor in body but rich in mind returned after having done useful work. Arrived in Calcutta by the 7.00 P. M. train. The last pie exhausted'. This shows how frugaly he spent in this tour, which lasted for about four months covering more than 1500 miles. Says a contemporary report, "he travelled as a pilgrim, not caring at all for comforts, mixing with the sanyasis, ascetics, Hindu pilgrims and with passengers of the third and intermediate classes, eating at time the poorest food, sleeping at time in places where the poor sleep and gaining an insight into the characteristics of the poor classes, who are suffering from intense ignorance, superstition and poverty".

A study of the diary leaves of Dharmapala of this tour makes an interesting reading. In particular, his comments on the caste distinctions are very pertinent and serve as an eye opener. He says :

"Oh the horrid caste system that keeps the 100 millions of the so-called low castes in eternal slavery." Again, "Oh the sight of the 'low caste' is painful". And again, "Oh when will that day of emancipation come for these down-trodden millions." And yet again, "Such is the fallen condition of the Indian people today. Caste distinctions everywhere. The highest Religion of India is Caste". And lastly he melancholy says : "India, the land of the Buddha, forgotten by his followers. When will I see again the Dharma in this land."

Soon after his whirl-wind tour of North India, Dharmapala received an invitation to visit Madras, where he not only lectured but also opened a branch of the Maha Bodhi Society in the year 1900 with the help of Prof. P. Lakshmi Narasu. Thus Buddhism came to life in the South also. The year 1900 also witnessed the opening of a branch of the Maha Bodhi Society at Kusinara, the site of Buddha's Mahaparinirvana where Mahavir Swami, the first modern Indian Bhikkhu had settled, and brought the deserted shrine to life. The year 1900 also saw the construction of a Dharmashala, at Bodh Gaya for the pilgrims. On a request made by Dharmapala the District Board of Gaya had agreed to construct a Rest House for the pilgrims visiting Buddha Gaya provided the cost thereof was met by the Maha Bodhi Society. In order to raise funds for this purpose, therefore, Dharmapala visited Burma and Ceylon in the early part of the year 1900.

Having gained a little foothold at Buddha Gaya with the construction of the Rest House, Dharmapala turned his eyes to Sarnath. In 1901, i.e. exactly ten years after his first visit to Sarnath, he purchased a plot of land there with Rs. 600/- donated by his mother.

In August 1902, Dharmapala sailed for the fourth time for the East and the United States of America. He came back to India in 1904 after doing useful Dhamma work in America, England, France and Italy. Then he concentrated his attention on the development of Sarnath; where he purchased some more plots; constructed a small living accommodation and also established a free Industrial School, largely with the donations from Mrs. Foster.

Dharmapala's battle against the mighty Mahant of Bodh Gaya received set back in 1906 when Mahant's suit for the ejection of the Buddhist monks from the Burmese Rest House on the plea that the Rest House was his property, was accepted by the District Court. As the High Court also upheld the lower court's judgement, the Maha Bodhi Society was temporarily ousted from the Rest House. Undaunted, however, Dharmapala continued the struggle.

Another set back in 1906 was the death of Dharmapala's father, who since 1891 had given unstinted financial support to his son. When this sad news reached Mrs Foster she at once wrote to Dharmapala to regard her as his foster mother, and also promised financial support. With her liberal donations, therefore, Dharmapala was able to establish a chain of Buddhist schools, a printing press, and a weekly in the Sinhalese language. called the Sinhala Bauddhaya. This paper became a major instrument for his missionary work in Sri Lanka.

In 1908, the Maha Bodhi Society got its permanent home in Calcutta when Dharmapala purchased a house with the liberal donation of 1,000 dollars sent by Mrs. Foster. Thus the headquarters of the Society were shifted from the rented accommodation at Creek Row to 4/A College Square in that year. Anagarika Dharmapala made another voyage round the world during the years 1913-14 visiting Burma, Thailand, China, Korea and Hawaii. At Honolulu, Dharmapala thanked personally Mrs. Foster for her magnificent support over the years. The good old lady was so much pleased to see the Anagarika and to hear the good use to which the money was being put that she gave him another sixty thousand rupees. With this amount, Dharmapala established in Colombo, a charitable hospital in memory of Mrs. Foster's father. The Foster Robinson Hospital was opened in a house inherited by Dharmapala from his father.

The first world war, which broke out in 1914, seriously hampered the activities of the Maha Bodhi Society as Dharmapala was interned by the British Government for five years in Calcutta at the request of the Government of Ceylon. Even during this forced confinement to one place, Dharmapala continued to work for the Dhamma, largely through the Maha Bodhi journal. In 1915, the Maha Bodhi Society of India was registered and Sir Ashutosh Mookerjee was elected its President in 1916 which post he continued to hold till his death in 1924. A major achievement of Dharmapala of this period was the construction of the beautiful Dharmarajika Vihara at Calcutta. It was in 1914 that he had secured a plot of land in the College Square at a cost of Rs. 20,000/- which was made up of Rs. '0,000/- from Anagarika's own savings, Rs. 9,000/- from Mrs. Foster and the balance from a few Sinhalese devotees. The foundation stone of this Vihara was laid in December 1918. The plan of this magnificent Vihara was prepared by Sir John Marshal on the model of the Ajanta Cave Temple, and M. M. Ganguly, the author of the Orissan Architecture, supervised the construction work. The total cost of the Vihara came to more than Rs. 1,10,000/-, out of which Mrs. Foster paid Rs. 88,000/-, and the balance was donated by the Maharaja of Baroda, Birla Brothers and few others from Calcutta and Ceylon. The opening ceremony of the Dharmarajika Vihara was performed on 20 November 1920 by His Excellency, Lord Ronaldshay, the Governor of Bengal. On the same day the sacred relics of the Buddha, discovered in a rock crystal casket during the excavations at Bhattiprolu in Andhra Pradesh by Mr. Rea in 1891, and gifted by the Government of India to the Maha Bodhi Society, were enshrined in this Vihara. Since its construction, the Dharmarajika Vihara has served as a beacon light in the movement of Buddhist revival in India.

After the completion of the Dharmarajika Vihara, the Anagarika again turned his eyes to Sarnath where he also wanted to build a beautiful Vihara. In 1917, he had purchased th re ten bighas of land with the amount of Rs 2,000/- donated by the Raja of Bhigna. The foundation stone of the Mulagandhakuti Vihara, the life of new Sarnath, the Holy Isipatana, was laid on 3 November 1922 by H. E. Sir Harcourt Butler, the Governor of U.P. The name 'Mulagandhakuti' was chosen as the first monastery in which Lord Buddha actually resided at Sarnath was known by that name.

During the artchaeological excavations at Sarnath a piece of tablet was also found on which this name was inscribed. This discovery prompted Anagarika Dharmapala to name the new Vihara as 'Mulagandhakuti' Vihara. Soon after the construction work of the Vihara had started, the Archaeological Survey of India objected to the site of the new Vihara. The work was, therefore, suspended, and remained so for the next four years. The dispute was ultimately settled in 1926; the Government having offered a suitable alternative plot for the Vihara as well as compensation to the Society for the expenditure already incurred on the foundation work. The Archaeological Survey of India also agreed to set apart about 20 acres of land and to develop the same as a park at their cost as an annexe to the Vihara. The negotiations, on behalf of the Society were carried by Dr. C.A. Hewavitarne, brother of Dharmapala, and Devapriya Valisinha. After this hurdle was crossed, the construction of the Vihara was started again in 1927, and completed in 1931. The magnificent Mulagandhakuti Vihara. with ancient Buddhist architectural decorations carved on red stone, cost about Rs. 1,20,000/- out of which Rs 30,000/- came from Mrs. Foster, Rs. 10,000/- from Government by way of compensation for the foundation work done by the Society at the earlier site, and balance was collected by the Sarnath Vihara Committee from the other well-wishers of Buddhism.

Coming to the other activities of Anagarika during this period, he toured Punjab and Kashmir again in 1924 on the invitation of Pandit Sheo Narain, a leading advocate of the Punjab High Court, Lahore In 1924, Sir Manmatha Nath Mukherji was elected President of the Maha Bodhi Society. In 1925, Dharmapala made another extensive tour of Ceylon and then left for London in 1926 where he established a branch of the Maha Bodhi Society and launched missionary work there for which Mrs. Foster gave him over fifty thousand rupees. Today, there stands the London Buddhist Vihara at Chiswick as a monument to the pioneer efforts of Dharmapala.

In 1929, Dharmapala returned to Ceylon and fell seriously ill. For the next three years he was confined to bed with stomach trouble and heart disease. In the meanwhile, his only surviving brother, Dr. C.A. Hewavitarne, who was of great help to him after the demise of his father, died in a tragic railway accident in 1929.

Then in December 1930, his foster mother, Mrs. Mary E. Foster, passed away. For Anagarika's living, the main financial support came from his family—father, mother and brothers - and for his other activities, particularly the buildings, his greatest benefactor was Mrs. Foster of Honolulu, who has often been ranked with Anathapindka and Visakha of Buddha's time. By the time, Mrs. Foster breathed her last in 1930, at the age of 86, her contributions to the Maha Bodhi Society had reached a total of ten lakh rupees. Mrs. Foster was an Ideal donor. Even in death she did not forget the sacred cause of Buddhism and left $ 50,000/- for the maintenance of the Foster Schools and Hospitals in India and Sri Lanka. The deaths of Mrs. Foster, and of his own brother, were a great loss for Dharmapala.

Inspite of these irreparable lossess, Dharmapala through sheer will-power recovered enough to undertake sea journey to Calcutta. At the end of March 1931, he reached Sarnath and began directing the affairs of the Society once again. He also brought to Sarnath a batch of ten samaneras from Sri Lanka, who he thought after training would be able to continue his efforts of propagating the Dhamma in India. Of these samaneras, two, namely Ven. Sangharatana and Ven. Dhammaratana, are more prominent. They dedicated their lives to the cause of Dhamma in India and fulfilled some of his dreams. Three samaneras from Chittagong were also taken. One of them, Ven L. Ariyawansa, being now at the Society's Delhi office.

Having spent his entire life as Anagarika or homeless wanderer, Dharmapala decided to take a step further on the road to Nirvana. On 13 July 1931 he took the Pabbajja or lower ordination from Ven. Boruggamuwe Rewata Thera and received the name of Sri Devamitta Dhammapala as Bhikkhu. Anagarika Dharmapala completed his life-long mission by consecrating the magnificent Mulagandhakuti Vihara at Sarnath on 11 November 1931 (Kartika Purnima). On the same day, the sacred relics of Lord Buddha, which were discovered by Sir John Marshal from Taxila, Punjab, in 1913-14, were presented by the Director General of Archaeology, Rai Bahadur Dayaram Sahni, to the Maha Bodhi Society on behalf of the Government of India and enshrined in a vault underneath the pedestal of the image in the Vihara.

The opening of the Mulagandhakuti Vihara was an important milestone in the history of modern Buddhism. Its completion was also the most glorious achievement of Anagarika Dharmapala, after 40 years of his labours for the revival of Buddhism in India.

The beautiful Ajanta style frescoes in the Mulagandhakuti Vihara were painted by the famous Japanese, artist, Kotesu Nosu, who spent about three years in executing the work in 1932-35. A British Buddhist, B. L. Broughton, who donated Rs 10,000/- was the chief donor for this splendid work of beautifying the Vihara.

In December 1932, Dharmapala again fell seriously ill, and wishing to die as a full member of the Sangha he received the Upasampada or higher ordination on 16 January 1933. More than a dozen venerable monks from Sri Lanka performed the ceremony which took place in a Seema specially consecrated for this purpose at Sarnath. Prior to that, he made Devapriya Valisinha, his most devoted and trusted assistant, the General Secretary and Treasurer of the Society in his place. On receiving higher ordination, Dharmapala felt greatly relieved of all the worries, and looked serene and calm. But within a couple of months his health took a serious turn and he breathed his last on 29 April 1933. His last wish was to take rebirth in India in order to accomplish his unfinished 'Dhamma work' in the land of the Buddha.

Thanks to the missionary zeal, devotion and dedication of Dharmapala, Buddhism once again came to life in India, and made significant progress in all the fields during the first forty years (1891-1931) of the revival movement. The achievements of Anagarika Dharmapala can be better summed up in the words of Ven Sangharakshita : "He stood not merely for the revival of Buddhism in Ceylon, where it had been weakened for centuries, but for its renaissance in India, where it had been dead for a millennium. This was indeed an astounding idea, and one which could have occurred only to a man of exceptional spiritual and outstanding courage. To revive in the land of its birth a religion that had been dead there a thousand years ! 'The impracticable dream of a young idealist !' scoffed his contemporaries. But undeterred Dharmapala set to work, fought vigorously to rescue Buddha Gaya reclaimed the sacred places, established centres, and kept up a continuous stream of propaganda with the result that before his death he was able to plant, and see beginning to sprout, the seed that is now fast growing into a noble tree".

2

DEVAPRIYA VALISINHA

Devapriya Valisinha a worthy disciple and successor of Anagarika Dharmapala, was born in Apalatotuwa, a village near Kandy in Sri Lanka, on 10 February 1904. He was the sixth child of a family of seven brothers and sisters. He lost both his parents at a tender age. His grandfather looked after him and his other brothers and sisters. A chance meeting in a Vihara in 1912 with Dharmapala, the founder of the Maha Bodhi Society of India. changed the course of the life of Valisinha. In the course of a lecture tour in that year Anagarika Dharmapala visited Udugama Vihara, situated halfway between Valisinha's school at Pindeniya and his village, for giving a lecture. Alongwith many other students, Valisinha also went to hear that lecture. While Valisinha was listening attentively to the lecture, Dharmapala kept on looking at him as he spoke. After the lecture, Dharmapala turned to him and asked if he was willing to go with him and work for the Dhamma. Without hesitation, Valisinha said that he was willing. Heartened by his spontaneous response, Dharmapala sought consent of his grandfather, who was also present there, to take Valisinha to Colombo to be educated at his own expense. After a family meeting, his grandfather gave his consent the next day. And without much preparation, Valisinha left Kandy for Colombo in pursuit of learning and subsequent service to humanity. For the next five years, he studied at Colombo and was under the loving care of Dharmapala's mother, Mallika Hewavitarne.

In 1917. Dharmapala asked his mother who was coming to India on pilgrimage to bring Valisinha with her to India. On coming to Calcutta, he was sent for further studies to the Ashram of Gurudev Rabindranath Tagore at Santiniketan. At that time Dharmapala had none to help him even in keeping accounts of the Society. And when he decided to build the Sri Dharmarajika Vihara, the need for assistance became more urgent. Therefore,

Valisinha had to leave Santiniketan after a year in order to serve his Master. On his return to Calcutta, he attended the Mitra Institution, at the same time helping, as far as possible, Dharmapala in the multifarious activities of the Society. In 1921, Valisinha passed Matriculation with distinction and joined the Presidency College from where he passed his B. A. in 1926. Even as a student, Valisinha was entrusted with almost all responsible work of the Society. And whenever, Dharmapala was on tour abroad in connection with his missionary work, Valisinha used to edit the Maha Bodhi journal and also look after all other affairs of the Society. Thus he began to gain experience in the Dhamma work.

In 1922, when Dharmapala was away in Sri Lanka, Valisinha alongwsth Ven. K. Srinivasa Nayaka Thera attended the Gaya Congress Session in order to bring to the notice of the delegates the problem of the Buddha Gaya Temple. Here he met for the first time Rahul Sankrityayan (then known as Baba Ramodardas) who, being a member of the Bihar Provincial Congress Committee, played a leading role in getting the Temple question taken up by the Congress Later, when an Enquiry Committee to go into the Buddha Gaya Temple question was appointed by the Congress under the Chairmanship of Dr. Rajendra Prasad, Valisinha and P. P. Siriwardene represented the Society on the Committee. Ultimately nothing came out of this Committee's report as even the mild recommendation that equal number of Buddhists and Hindus should manage the Temple was not accepted by the Mahant.

Another problem which had to be handled by Valisinha at this time was the construction of the Mulagandhakuti Vihara at Sarnath The foundation stone of the Vihara was laid in November 1922. The site was near the Dhamek Stupa. When the foundation had come up to the ground level, the Archaeological Survey of India objected to the siting of the proposed Vihara so close to the Dhamek Stupa and brought an injunction against the Society. Thus the construction work had to be suspended. In order to sort out this problem, Valisinha had to run up and down between Calcutta and Sarnath even at the cost of his studies. Ultimately, he and Dr. C.A Hewavitarne, brother of Anagarika Dharmapala, met Sir John Marshall at Taxila and persuaded him to allot another plot for the Vihara and also to compensate the Society for the work already done. Thus after a gap of four years; the construction work started again in 1927 at the new site under the supervision of Valisinha. He was mainly responsible for introducing the stone facing of the Mulagandhakuti Vihara as he felt that a brick building, as originally planned would not be harmonious with the surroundings. While the construction work was going on, Dharmapala who had just returned from England after starting a Buddhist Mission in London, decided to send three Bhikkhus to England. Valisinha was chosen as the Manager and he accompanied the Bhikkhus in 1928 to London. There, while doing the Dhamma work, Valisinha also joined the School of Oriental Studies, London and studied Buddhism for about two years.

On retnrn to India in 1930, Valisinha resumed his duties as Recording Secretary of the Society, the post to which he had been appointed in 1927. He also took over the supervision work of the Mulagandhakuti Vihara from Siriwardene who was looking after the work in his absence Thus Valisinha saw the completion of the Vihara and started making preparations for its opening in a befitting manner. After the consecration of the prestigious Mulagandhakuti Vihara on 11 November 1931, Valisinha thought of making Sarnath a living centre of Buddhism. With the blessings of Anagarika Dharmapala, who was by now a sickly person, Valisinha started at Sarnath the Maha Bodhi Vidyalaya, as well as a Free Dispensary. These institutions proved a boon for the people of the villages around Sarnath. Valisinha also started the Dharmaduta, a Hindi monthly for propagating Buddhism amongst the masses. He also organised the Vihara Library to which books were gifted by Pandit Sheo Narain of Lahore and C.S. Strauss of New York. He was also instrumental in getting a donation of Rs. 10,000/- from B.L. Broughton, a British Buddhist, with which marvellous paintings in the Mulagandhakuti Vihara were completed by a Japanese artist.

Valisinha was the most devoted and trusted assistant of Dharmapala. In fact, he was to the Anagarika what Ananda was to the Buddha. No wonder, before receiving higher ordination as a Bhikkhu on 16 January 1933, Anagarika Dharmapala appointed Valisinha as General Secretary and Treasurer of the Society in his place. Three months later, Dharmapala passed away on 29 April 1933 leaving behind the burden and responsibility of running the Maha Bodhi Society to Devapriya Valisinha. For the next 35 years, from 1933 to 1968, Valisinha held the post of General Secretary of the Maha Bodhi Society of India. As a result of his hard work, devotion and dedication, the Society during this period grew from strength to strength and expanded its activities in all the directions.

From the very beginning, the publication of Buddhist literature became a favourite activity of Valisinha. In 1933-35 itself, he published Dhammapada, Vinaya Pitaka, Digha Nikaya, Majjhima Nikaya, translated from Pali into Hindi by Rahul Sankrityayan. These were followed by other important books in Hindi and English written by eminent Buddhist savants. Besides editing, with great love and care the Maha Bodhi journal, he himself also wrote and published books like 'Buddhist Shrines in India' and 'A Guide to Buddha Gaya' for the benefit of the pilgrims visiting Buddhist sacred shrines. Availability of this literature helped a lot in disseminating correct information about Buddhism and Buddhist heritage.

The opening of the Mulagandhakuti Vihara at Sarnath, and the subsequent annual function held there in November every year attracted pilgrims to Sarnath in large numbers. As the need for providing some accommodation for the pilgrims became acute, Valisinha began looking for a donor who could finance such a project. As a result, Seth Jugal Kishore Birla of Pilani came forward to build a Dharmashala (Rest House) at Sarnath ; the foundation stone of which was laid in December 1934. Later, the persuasive power of Valisinha induced Birlaji to finance the construction of a similar Dharmashala at Kushinagar.

In 1934, Valisinha attended the Pan-Pacific Buddhists Conference held in Tokyo and was elected its senior Vice-President, While in Japan he gave several lectures on Buddhism and the Society's missionary activities. On his way back to India, he also addressed gatherings in Hongkong, Shangai, Singapore and Penang. In 1938 Valisinha took a long tour of Burma, Singapore, Malaya and Hongkong. He thus renewed the cultural relations with these countries which Anagarika Dharmapala, the founder of the Maha Bodhi Society had established earlier.

At the outbreak of the Japanese War in 1941 Valisinha was arrested by the British Government. He fell ill in the jail and was released On his release, he was taken to Ceylon for treatment by his friend Raja Hewavitarne. As soon as Valisinha reached Colombo, he was served with a notice not to return to India till the end of the second world war. Thus perforce he had to spend five years in Ceylon. Undaunted he utilised this period to put the Maha Bodhi Society of Ceylon, of which also he was General Secretary, in order. He went round the Island and raised over Rs. 1.25 lakhs. With this amount, the Colombo Headquarters Building, and the premises of the Madras Maha Bodhi Society at Kennet Lane were purchased.

Valisinha also built two new Buddha Viharas which enhanced the prestige of the Maha Bodhi Society ; these being one at New Delhi and the other at Sanchi. The land for the Vihara in New Delhi, the Capital of India, was acquired by one Sarbananda Barua and donated to the Maha Bodhi Society. While endeavouring to raise the required funds, Valisinha put up a signboard on the land on the Reading Road (now Mandir Marg) saying 'Site for Buddhist Temple". On seeing the board, Seth J.K. Birla, who was a great philanthropist, enquired from Valisinha as to who had obtained the land. When told that it was for the Maha Bodhi Society, he gladly agreed to bear the entire cost of the Vihara and other buildings. When built, this Vihara was opened by Mahatma Gandhi on 18 March 1939. Being in the heart of New Delhi, this modest stone built Vihara serves almost like an International Temple of Understanding catering to the needs of the Buddhists from all parts of the world.

One of the greatest achievements of Valisinha was to seek return of the Relics of Sariputta and Moggallana, the two chief disciples of the Buddha, from London and their restoration at their original resting place, Sanchi,. These relics consisting of one small bone-relic of Sariputta and two of Moggallana, together with seven beads of pearl, lapis lazuli and crystal, representing the Seven Precious Objects that were always deposited with holy relics, were discovered by Sir Alexander Cunningham in 1851 from the third Stupa at Sanchi Hill and were taken to London where they were kept in safe custody in the Victoria and Albert Museum. The first effort to get back these precious relics was made in 1933 by the Maha Bodhi Society's London Centre, In that year, a deputation led by Bhadant Anand Kausalyayan, who was then incharge of the London Centre, approached the Curator of the Victoria and Albert Museum requesting for the return of the relics. The Curator was sympathetic, but as he had no power to act in the matter without the consent of the British Government, he advised the delegation to approach the Government. He, however, permitted a party of Buddhists to worship the relics in the Museum, and this was done with traditional Buddhist ceremonies on the Full Moon Day of November 1933. The matter rested there until 1938, when Valisinha approached the Museum, through the Government of India, for the return of the said Relics. The Government of U.K. consented to hand over the Relics to the Maha Bodhi Society to be enshrined in the newly constructed Buddha Vihara in New Delhi. Then the second world war intervened and the transfer was postponed.

In the meanwhile, the Government of Bhopal very generously offered assistance to the Society in building a worthy Temple at Sanchi itself to enshrine these Relics. Accordingly, the foundation stone of the new Cetiyagiri Vihara was laid on 8 January 1946 by His Highness the Nawab of Bhopal. The cost of the Vihara was borne jointly by the Maha Bodhi Societies of India and Ceylon. The Nawab of Bhopal also contributed Rs. 25,000/- besides giving land, some building material and technical staff for supervising the construction work. When the war ended, the matter was again taken up with the British Government. And on 20 February 1947, the sacred Relics were handed over by the Museum to Daya Hewavitarne, a nephew of Anagarika Dharmapala, who was deputed by the Maha Bodhi Society and the Government of India for this purpose. As per arrangement, the Relics were first taken to Sri Lanka and Burma for exposition. Finally, the Relics arrived in India on 13 February 1949, and were handed over to the Maha Bodhi Society of India by Jawaharlal Nehru, Prime Minister of India, at a public function held on 14 January 1949. The sacred Relics of Sariputta and Moggallana after exposition in the country at several places, were enshrined at Sanchi, in the new Cetiyagiri Vihara, in November 1952, in the presence of the Prime Ministers of India (Nehru) and Burma (U NU). With the restoration of these Relics, Sanchi again came to life and became one of the most sacred Buddhist Shrines.

The Maha Bodhi Society, under the stewardship of Valisinha, also took over the management of three Viharas built by the other pioneers of the revival movement. These Viharas were handed over by their builders to the Society as they thought that the Maha Bodhi Society was in a better position to manage them. The first Vihara to be taken over by the Society was the Bahujana Vihara built by Dharmananda Kosambi in 1937 at Parel in Bombay. Later, the Ananda Vihara built in Bombay in 1931 by Dr. A.L. Nair was taken over by the Society. The third Vihara to be taken over by the Society was the one at Lucknow built in 1925 by Ven. Bodhananda. It was taken over in 1952.

Another great achievement of Valisinha was the passage of the Buddha Gaya Management Act 1949 in accordance with which the Buddhists gained partial control on the Maha Bodhi Temple. Ever since 1922, Valisinha had been associated with the movement for regaining this holy temple from the Mahant. He kept on raising this question at every forum which he thought could help in finding a solution. In 1935, he attended the Kanpur Session of the Hindu Maha Sabha presided over by Bhikkhu Ottama of Burma and raised this question in the Subjects Committee. After a great deal of hesitation, an Enquiry Committee was appointed. Valisinha and G.K.W. Perera of Ceylon appeared before the Committee. This Enquiry Committee also recommended the appointment of a Joint Managing Committee. The Mahant left the decision to the Shankaracharya of Puri, who vehemently opposed the recommendations and the matter rested where it was. Subsequently, when India became free, Valisinha pursued the matter with the Bihar Government. And as a result of the co-operation of Dr. Srikrishana Sinha and Dr. Rajendra Prasad, the 1949 Act was passed transferring management to a committee of four Buddhists and four Hindus with the District Magistrate of Gaya as Chairman. Though not a very happy solution yet it was something of an achievement for which the Buddhists had to struggle for nearly sixty years. Among the four Buddhists nominated to the first Board of Management constituted in 1952, Valisinha was one. He continued to hold this position till his death.

Valisinha was also primarily responsible for the 2500th Buddha Jayanti Celebrations being organised by the Government of India. Much before the historic celebrations in 1956 he had started publicising this event. He also wrote to the Government of India and the State Governments to celebrate the event in a worthy manner. He also personally met the Prime Minister of India, Jawaharlal Nehru and placed before him a list of items for consideration as part of the celebrations, such as, publication of the Tripitika, a book in English '2500 Years of Buddhism", improvement of Buddhist sacred shrines, issue of special postage stamp to commemmorate the event. Later, the Maharaj Kumar of Sikkim, who was then the President of the Maha Bodhi Society, also met the Prime Minister and renewed the request. The Prime Minister responded graciously and the Government of India while agreeing to most of the suggestions made by Valisinha decided to implement the suggestions regarding improvement of approaches to the sacred places, publication of books etc., Accordingly, a Buddha Jayanti Celebrations Committee was set up by the Government of India with Dr. S. Radhakrishnan, the Vice-President of India, as its Chairman. The Maharaj Kumar of Sikkim was one of the Members of this Committee, and Valisinha was an alternate Member. Valisinha, therefore, attended several meetings of the Committee and saw with satisfaction concretisation of his ideas when the Government of India and the various State Governments organised the year long celebrations in a befitting manner.

An important event of the year 1956 was the home-coming of the Sacred Relics of Arhat Moggaliputta Tissa and nine other Arhats who lived at the time of Asoka. These Relics were in the possession of the British Museum, London, where they were taken in 1851. These Relics were brought back on February 5, 1956 by Shrimati Vijaya Lakshmi Pandit, Indian High Commissioner in U.K. and were received at Delhi Airport at a colourful function by Prime Minister Nehru. The first casket containing the Relics of Moggaliputta, Kosikiputta and Gotiputta was presented by the Government of India to the Government of Ceylon. The other two caskets containing the Relics of Mahavanya, Apagira Kodiniputta, Vachiya-Savijayata, Kasapa-gota, Majhima and Haritiputta were presented to the Maha Bodhi Society of India who enshrined them in the Cetiyagiri Vihara at Sanchi.

Devapriya Valisinha was well-known to Dr. B.R. Ambedkar, and in fact had specifically requested him in 1950 to contribute an article to the Maha Bodhi journal. When Dr Ambedkar decided to embrace Boddhism, Valisinha was the happiest man. He was present at the historic Deeksha ceremony at Nagpur on 14 October 1956 and welcomed the great leader to the Buddhist fold by presenting to him an image of the Buddha. Significantly enough, Valisinha was instrumental in arranging a donation for the first Buddha Vihara at Nagpur. The foundation stone of this pioneer Vihara at Nagpur. was laid on 14 April 1957 by Mrs. N. Y. Sandup, a devout lady of Darjeeling, who, on a suggestion made by Valisinha, had graciously agreed to donate Rs. 5,000/- for the purpose. Ven. Bhadant Anand Kausalyayan presided over the function which was organised of the Bhartiya Baudh Maha Sabha. Valisinha addressed the gathering and exhorted the Buddhists to follow the example set by Babasaheb Ambedkar. After this function, Valisinha addressed a series of meetings at Nagpur, Wardha and surrounding villages on 15-16 April. Then he left for Bombay where he addressed half a dozen meetings of the Buddhists on 18-19 April 1957. Thus Valisinha took an active part in the new movement initiated by Dr. Ambedkar. In order to give impetus to the movement, he also opened the 'Indian Buddhist Fund', and arranged to publish over 50,000 copies of a booklet in Hindi and Marathi on Buddhist worship and allied matters for free distribution amongst the new Buddhists. Over a dozen persons from amongst the new Buddhists were also ordained and given training at Sarnath with the help of this fund. Valisinha continued to help in various ways the new movement in subsequent years also.

Ever since the inception of the World Fellowship of Buddhists, Valisinha was associated with it and was more than once elected its Vice-President. He attended all the meetings of the W.F.B. from 1950 onward; the last being in 1964 at Sarnath which he organised there as part of the Anagarika Dharmapala Birth Cenetenary Celebrations. In 1954, Valisinha was invited by the Buddhists of Japan to attend the World Pacificist Conference held in Tokyo and other towns in Japan. In 1958, he visited Thailand, Cambodia and Laos and gave a number of lectures on Buddhism. In 1959, Valisinha again visited Japan to participate in the 2500th Buddha Jayanti Celebrations and the Cultural Conference organised there on the occasion. As a result of his contracts all over the world, the Maha Bodhi Society became an important international Buddhist organisation.

In his capacity as General Secretary of the Maha Bodhi Society for over three decades, Valisinha did a marvellous job. But for his untiring zeal and devotion to the Buddha-Dhamma, the mission of Anagarika Dharmapala, his Guru, might have failed Thanks to Valisinha's vision, the Maha Bodhi Society has now a chain of centres, Viharas and educational institutions working for the cause of Buddhism in India and abroad. The last great event in the life of such a dedicated servant of the Dhamma was the Dharmapala Cenetenary celebrations in 1964-65 Soon after the celebrations were over, Valisinha had an attack of paralysis on 18 December 1965. Inspite of best medical treatment, he did not recover. On 1st may 1968, he was taken to Sri Lanka for further treatment. There he passed away in a Colombo Hospital on 3 August 1968.

3

VEN. K. SIRINIWASA

Venerable K. Siriniwasa Nayaka Thera was born in Sri Lanka in 1891. He was ordained as Samanera in 1900 and received his Dhamma education at the Vidoyodaya Pirivena (now a University) in Sri Lanka. At the invitation of Anagarika Dharmapala, he came to India in 1920 and began his missionary work with the Maha Bodhi Society. He helped the Anagarika in the construction of Sri Dharmarajika Vihara, Calcutta and the Mulagandhakuti Vihara, Sarnath. At Sarnath he also built several "Kutis". For a long time he concentrated his missionary activities in the Sravasti-Lumbini region. and built Buddha Viharas and Rest Houses at Nowgarh and Balrampur for the convenience of the pilgrims.

Ven. Siriniwasa travelled extensively in India, Nepal and Burma. His life was a life of deep piety and simplicity. He was well-versed in Sinhalese, Sanskrit, Pali, Hindi and English, and was also an able and efficient preacher. He inspired many people to adopt the Buddhist way of life.

Having served the cause of Buddhism in India for over forty-eight years, Ven. Siriniwasa passed away, at the ripe age of 7[illegible], at Sarnath on 13 September 1968.

4

VEN. SASANASIRI

Venerable D. Sasanasiri Maha Nayaka Thera was born in 1899 in the Migmuv district Sri Lanka. He took Pabajja in 1914 and received the higher ordination (Upasampada) in 1920. He studied Pali and Tripitaka ot the famous Vidyodaya Pirivena, Colombo (now a University) from 1919 to 1929 graduating us "Prachin Scholar" and "Tripitakacharya". In 1929, Anagarika Dharmapala founder of the Maha Bodhi Society, requested him to come to India and train the Samaneras brought from Sri Lanka for serving the cause of Buddhism in India. Ven. Sasanasiri gladly accepted the invitation and came to Santiniketan where the Samaneras were getting education. In 1930, he came to Sarnath and was appointed the head of the newly established International Buddhist Institute (Dhammaduta Training School). Among this batch of Samaneras, trained by him, were : Ven. M. Sangharatana and Dr. U. Dham maratana. Thereafter, Ven. Sasanasiri was Bhikkhu in-charge of almost all the centres of the Maha Bodhi Society—Bombay, Buddha Gaya, Calcutta and New Delhi. Finally, he returned to Sarnath in 1949 and became a permanent resident of the holy Isipatana.

During his long service of 35 years of the Buddha-Dhamma in India, Ven. Sasanasiri ordained a number of Indian and foreign monks. Amongst his Indian disciples names of the Bhikkhus Katayayana, Rashtrapal, Vimalsheel, Shobhit, Vishudhanand, Bodhanand, Dharmakirti, Medhankar, and Sugatanand are noteworthy. Ven. Sasanasiri was also a great scholar and well-versed in Hindi, Sanskrit, Pali, Sinhalese and English languages. He had translated Ashvaghosha's Sanskrit treatise 'Bodhichariyavatara' into Sinhalese. His most important publication in Hindi was 'Buddh-ki-Den' published in 1960. At the time of his death on 30 October 1966, Ven. Sasanasiri was serving as Professor of Pali in the Dharmapala Degree College, Sarnath.

5

VEN. N. JINARATANA

Venerable Neluwe Jinaratana Nayaka Maha Thera was born on 17 March 1913 in a Jayawardane family at Neluwa, a remote village in the midst of hills, in District Galle in Sri Lanka. He was ordained as Samanera in 1929 by Ven. P. Vipulatissa Maha Thera at Pannagale Vihara, and received the higher ordination (Upasampada) at Malwatta Maha Vihara, Kandy in 1933. He had his Pirivena education in Sinhala, Pali and Sanskrit, passing the final examination in Oriental Studies in 1934. Coming to India in 1936 Ven. Jinaratana joined the Maha Bodhi Society as a Dhammaduta worker. Soon he became an important functionary of the Society. In 1938, he was appointed as the Bhikkhu-in-charge of the Sri Dharmarajika Vihara at Calcutta ; as Managing Editor of the Maha Bodhi Journal in 1942 ; Assistant Secretary of the Society in 1943 ; Joint Secretary in 1948 ; Trustee of the Society in 1952 ; and lastly General Secretary in 1968 following the demise of Davapriya Valisinha.

Besides looking after the day-to-day affairs of the Maha Bodhi Society and preaching Dhamma with zeal and devotion, Ven. Jinaratana took keen interest in social service. When in 1943 Bengal was ravaged by a severe famine, he did yeoman's service by organising relief work, and founded the Maha Bodhi Orphanage and Welfare Home for providing free education, boarding and lodging to poor and needy children. The five-storey building of the Maha Bodhi Welfare Home and Orphanage, Calcutta, constructed in 1960 at a cost of Rupees four lakhs is a living testimony to his abiding interest in human welfare.

As representative of the Maha Bodhi Society, Ven. Jinaratana participated in many National and International Conferences. He was a familiar figure at the World Fellowship of Buddhists as well as Conferences of the Asian Buddhist Council for Peace. Among other Conferences, he attended in 1966 the Asian Peace and Anti-

Nuclear Arms Congress held at Tokyo, Japan. He was also the Leader of the delegation to Japan carrying Sacred Relics of the Lord Buddha in 1966. Earlier he, alongwith Ven. Sangharatana, had accompanied the sacred relics of Sariputta and Moggallana Arahans to Burma, Nepal, Thailand, and Cambodia.

Ven. Jinaratana was also associated with several other Buddhist organisations—he was a Founder Member of the Asian Buddhist Council for Peace, one of the Founder Vice-Presidents of the International Buddhist Brotherhood Association of Japan, and a member of the Buddha Gaya Temple Management Committee. He was also associated with several academic bodies, including the Universities of Calcutta and Banaras.

In recognition of his services rendered to Buddhism, Ven. Jinaratana was honoured in 1958 by the Sangha Council of Malwatta Chapter of the Siamese Sect of Sri Lanka by conferring on him the title of Sangha Nayaka of India. He was also honoured by the educational institutions. An honorary degree of M.A. was conferred on him in 1960 by the Vidyodaya University of Sri Lanka. In 1976, an honorary degree of D. Litt. was conferred on him by the Nava Nalanda Maha Vihara, Nalanda.

During his tenure as General Secretary of the Maha Bodhi Society from 1968 to 1983, Ven. Jinaratana not only maintained tempo of the activities of the Society but added further strength to them. An important event successfully organised by him was the International Conference and Seminar on the Contribution of Buddhism to World Culture and Civilization in Vigyan Bhavan, New Delhi in March 1977 in commemmoration of the 2600th Birth Anniversary of the Buddha. He also made a notable addition to the assets of the Society by completing the building of the Dharmapala Institute of Culture and International Guest House. He further enhanced the prestige of the Society by opening new Centres of the Society in other parts of the world.

A true Buddhist missionary, always smiling kindhearted, full

of love and compassion for one and all, Ven. Jinaratana breathed his last on 9 November 1983 at Calcutta, where he had spent about half a century serving the cause of Buddhism in India. His last rites were performed on 13 November. His ashes were taken in a casket to Sri Lanka and laid to rest, with due honour, in a special receptacle constructed at the Pannagale Monastery where he had joined the Sangha 54 years earlier.

6

VEN. U. DHAMMARATANA

Ven. Dr. U. Dhammaratana, M.A. Ph.D., D. Litt. was born at Uruwala in Western province of Sri Lanka on 23 November 1917. Born in a devout Buddhist family, W.K. Jayasekara, as he was called in his childhood, often visited the Maligatenna hermitage along with his parents. Ven. M. Devananda Maha Thera, the then incumbent of the Vihara was well-known for his piety and clear exposition of the Dhamma Finding the young Jayasekara listening to discourses with keen interest, the Mahathera one day asked him whether he would be willing to join the Foster Buddhist Seminary started by Anagarika Dhamapala for imparting training to Dhammadutas for the propagation of Buddhism in India Without any hesitation. Jayasekara responded in the positive, and with the consent of his parents, he joined the Foster Buddhist Seminary in Kandy in 1928. He was ordained as Samanera by Ven. M. Devananda Maha Thera, and given the new name of Uruwala Dhammaratana.

In 1931, Anagarika Dharmapala brought a batch of ten Samaneras from Sri Lanka for training. Ven. Dhammaratana was the youngest member among these Samaneras On arrival in India they were first of all sent to Santiniketan for studies Later, when the Mulagandhakuti Vihara was opened in November 1931, they were brought to Sarnath for further education where arrangements had been made for this purpose. At Sarnath, they were instructed in Dhamma and Vinaya under the joint preceptorship of Venerable D. Sasanasiri and Venerable H. Dhammaloka. Anagarika B. Govinda used to give them lessons in western philosophy. After the passing away of Anagarika Dharmapala in April 1933, however, special classes organised at Sarnath did not continue for long. Faced with this problem, Ven. Dhammaratana decided to follow a systematic academic course Accordingly, he went to Calcutta to pursue the studies. In due course, he graduated from the Calcutta University. Later, he pursued his post-graduate studies in Pali and Philosophy at the Banaras Hindu University with the kind help of Ven. Jagdish Kashyap who had joined the B.H.U. as a teacher of Pali, and was staying in the Buddhakuti specially built for him by Seth Jugal Kishore Birla. After completing his post-graduate studies, Ven. Dhammaratana made Sarnath the centre of his activities. He edited for some ten years the Hindi journal 'Dharmaduta' published by the Maha Bodhi Society from Sarnath. During this period, he also wrote several books on Buddhism in Hindi and English. Besides writing Visuddhimagga Ki Ruparekha, he translated into Hindi Theragatha, Suttanipata, Khuddakapatha. His English works written during this period were : The Buddha and Caste-System, A Study of Patisambhida-magga, An Introduction to Visuddhi-magga. The Buddha and His Message.

When in 1956, in connection with the 2500th Buddha Jayanti Celebrations, a project was prepared jointly by the Government of Bihar and Government of India to publish a complete edition of the Pali Tripitaka under the auspices of Nava Nalanda Maha Vihara, Nalanda, and Ven. Jagdish Kashyap was appointed Editor-in-Chief, he invited Ven Dhammaratana to join the project. In the meanwhile, Ven. Dhammaratana was awarded the degree of Ph.D. by the University of Calcutta for his thesis 'A Comparative Study of the Anatta Doctrine in Pali Nikayas and that of the Madhyamika System of Nagarjuna'. Consequently, he was appointed as a Lecturer in Pali and Philosophy. Later on, he was promoted as Professor of Pali and Philosophy. In view of his vast knowledge and amiable behaviour, he was very popular with the students and research scholars who came in contact with him. He also served as Research Examiner in Buddhist studies in several Universities, such as, Delhi, Banaras, Lucknow, Santiniketan, and Colombo. In recognition of his services to Buddhism, he was awarded an honorary degree of D. Litt. by the Nava Nalanda Mahavihara.

Ven. U. Dhammaratana was for many years associated with the editoral team of the Maha Bodhi journal, the English monthly published by the Maha Bodhi Society of India from Calcutta. After the passing away of Devapriya Valisinha, he was appointed as Editor of that journal, and also Joint Secretary of the Maha

Bodhi Society. Even while performing this dual responsibility, he generally stayed at Nalanda or at Sarnath as he felt more at home at these places. Being a practitioner, Ven. Dhammaratana took keen interest in the Vipassana Meditation Camps, specially those conducted by Acharya S.N. Goenka. After his retirement from the Nava Nalanda Mahavihara, he devoted more and more his time and energy in spreading the message of the Buddha in India and many other countries which he visited including U.K., U.S.A, Canada, and Japan where he delivered Dhamma discourses and conducted Vipassana meditation camps.

After the passing away of Ven. N. Jinaratana Nayaka Maha Thera, Ven. Dr. U. Dhammaratana was elected as General Secretary of the Maha Bodhi Secretary of India in 1983 but he could not continue for long due to his failing health. He, therefore, resigned and came to Buddha Gaya Maha Bodhi Society Centre for rest. Soon he fell ill there, and came to Lucknow for treatment After thorough investigations, the physicians of the King George' Medical College found that he was suffering from Heart Disease which required Coronary Bypass Surgery, and advised him to go to U.K. or U.S.A. Consequently, with the benevolent help of some friends, he was taken to London on 10 June 1985. There he was operated upon on 8 July 1985. Unfortunately, inspite of best medical care, he breathed his last on 20 July 1985 As per the wish of his relatives, his body was taken to his native place in Sri Lanka for his last rites.

7

VEN. M. SANGHARATANA

Born in 1912 in Sri Lanka Venerable Metivala Sangharatana Maha Nayaka Thera came to India in 1927 He was one of the ten Samaneras selected in 1931 for Dhammaduta work in India by Anagarika Dharmapala, the founder of the Maha Bodhi Society. He had his higher education at Santiniketan and learnt Dhamma under the able guidance of Ven. Sasanasiri Maha Nayaka Thera. In 1937. he was appointed as one of the Joint Secretaries of the Maha Bodhi Society and Bhikkhu-in-charge of the Mulagandhakuti Vihara, Sarnath. In this capacity, he served the Society dilligently and devotedly for more than three decades, and was chiefly responsible for making Sarnath a living holy shrine. Being an active Dhammaduta worker and an important functionary of the Maha Bodhi Society, he participated in many National and International Buddhist functions. Recognising his services to Buddhism, he was honoured in 1961 with a title of Sangha Nayaka of India by the Sangha Council of the Malwatta Chapter of Siamese Sect, Kandy, Sri Lanka.

Ven. Sangharatana, after retirement from the Maha Bodhi Society in 1969, came to live at Sravasti, the sacred place where the Buddha had spent 25 rainy seasons Though some improvements had been made at Sravasti at the time of 2500th Buddha Jayanti in 1956 yet the fortunes of Sravasti, the present day twin ruins of Sahet-Mahet, changed for the better only after the arrival of Ven. Sangharatana. As a results of his efforts, the Government of India fenced the old Jetavana Monastery and its surroundings, and also added a beautiful garden. His major contribution to the development of Sravasti is the construction of the Sri Lankaramaya Temple, and Rest House, with all modern facilities for the visiting pilgrims. Keen to make Sravasti an educational centre, he also opened a school under the aegis of the Bhartiya Baudha Shiksha Parishad, founded by him.

While engaged in this noble task of making Sravasti once again a living shrine, Ven. Sangharatana fell ill, and breathed his last in a Lucknow Hospital on 31 December, 1984 As per his last wish, his body was taken to Sravasti and cremated there in front of the sacred Jetavana on 2 January, 1985. Thus Ven. Sangharatana has become inseparable from Sravasti, and his name will echo for ever through the gardens of Jetavana.

8

VEN. U CHANDRAMANI

The task of making Kusinara a living shrine initiated by Ven. Mahavira was successfully accomplished by Venerable U Chandramani. He was born in Burma in June (Jyastha 6) in 1876, in a devout Buddhist family of a small village situated on the bank of river Raccho in Tehsil Morahau in district Akyab of Arakan province. At the age of seven, in 1883, he started his education under the Bhikkhu-incharge of the Buddha Vihara in the neighbouring village Rupaccho. From the very beginning, he was of calm and quiet nature, and loved solitude. In 1886, at the age of ten, he renounced his hearth and home, and came to live with his uncle Bhikkhu U Chandima who was residing in the city of Akyab. Two years later, in 1888, he was ordained as sramanera and was given the name 'Chanda' in place of his original name of 'Saba U' given by his parents.

When in 1891, Anagarika Dharmapala, the founder of the Maha Bodhi Society, requested Ven. U Chandima to send some suitable Dhammadutas for missionary work in India, he sent two sramaneras : Chanda and Surya to Calcutta. On arrival in India, Chanda or U Chandramani, as he later became famous, came to Bodh Gaya and started staying in the Burmese Rest House, where Anagarika Dharmapala had installed four Buddhist monks from Sri Lanka to look after the sacred Maha Bodhi Temple. The Hindu Mahant, who was then in occupation of the Temple, was unhappy with the presence of the Bhikkhus and wanted them to leave. It is said that one night he manipulated a dacoity in the Burmese Rest House, in the course of which the monks were beaten up. Horrified by this incident, Chanda went back to Burma in 1892. But he returned to Calcutta within a few months, in 1893, with a firm resolve to work for the revival of Buddhism in India, and started learning Indian languages while staying in a Dharmashala there. In 1895, he per chance met Ven. Mahavira at the residence of a Burmese Buddhist. Impressed by the keenness of the young sramanera, Ven. Mahavira made necessary arrangements for the studies of Chanda at the Sanskrit Paathshala at Khetipur near Gazipur in Bihar. The expenses involved in his studies were borne by Khezari Babu (Maung Khee Zarhee) of Burma, who was a worthy Dayaka of Ven. Mahavira. After completing his studies in Sanskrit, Chanda went back in 1899 to Burma for pursuing Pali studies. There, he studied Pali Tripitaka under the able guidance of the then renowned Pali scholars of Burma, and attained mastery in Pali and Buddhist philosophy While in Burma, he also received Upasampada (higher ordination) at the Ramu grama Vihara on the full-moon day of Magha in 1903. His Upajjhaya was his uncle Ven. U Chandima Maha Thera. Consequently, he was given the name of Bhikkhu U Chandramani. Thereafter, he came back to India and started living with Ven. Mahavira at Kushinagar.

At that time, the sacred Nirvana Temple at Kushinagar was in the possession of the Archaeological Survey of India, and there were no arrangements to worship the historic image of the Buddha. Ven. U Chandramani immediately took up the matter with the Government and managed to get its possession as well as permission to worship the sacred image. Thus the ancient Nirvana Temple once again became a living shrine in 1904. The 1500 year old Nirvana statue, which is an excellent piece of art, is 20 feet (6.1 m) in length and is executed out of one block of sandstone of mixed reddish colour, probably from chunar. It represents the Dying Buddha reclining on his right side with face turned towards the west An inscription of A.D 5th century on it records that the statue was the "appropriate religious gift of the Mahavihara-swamin Haribala and that it was fashioned by Dinna". The reclining Buddha image is believed to be on the very spot where Lord Buddha had breathed his last (attained Parinirvana). Its possession by Ven. Chandramani in 1904 was, therefore, a significant step in the Buddhist revival movement. And its worship by the Buddhists since then has made Kushinagar one of the most sacred shrines.

The arrival of Ven. Chandramani at Kushinagar as a resident monk further enhanced its popularity. As the number of pilgrims to Kushinagar increased, he constructed another Dharmashala for the convenience of the pilgrims And in order to disseminate the knowledge about Buddhism among the massess, Ven. Chandramani translated and published Dhammapada into Hindi. He also translated a number of Pali Suttas into Hindi and Burmese and published them in the shape of small pamphlets for wider circulation from time to time. Extending his activities to the other sacred shrines around Kushinagar, Ven. Chandramani constructed a Buddha Vihara at Sravasti ; a Dharmashala at Balrampur for the facility of pilgrims visiting Sravasti ; and a Buddha Vihara at Lumbini. He also constructed a Dharmashala at Sarnath for the convenience of the Burmese pilgrims.

After the demise of Ven. Mahavira in 1919, Ven. Chandramani continued the Dhamma work with more zeal and vigour. In 1924, he organised the Buddha Jayanti function for the first time at Kushinagar, and since then it is a regular feature. In 1927, he repaired and restored the Main Stupa, with the donations of U Po Kyo, a Burmese Buddhist. Inside the drum of this 75 feet high Stupa, a chamber, representing a miniature replica of the original stupa, was constructed at a height of 20 feet above the ground level. On 18 March 1927, this chamber was ceremoniously closed, in the presence of sixteen Buddhist monks, headed by Ven. U Chandramani. Numerous objects of gold, silver and copper, and a copper-plate inscription were deposited inside the Stupa recording the fact and circumstances of the discovery, indentification of the monument, and its restoration. The present Matha-Kuar Temple at Kushinagar was also built and consecrated by Ven. Chandramani. It was built in 1928 out of the donations of two Burmese Buddhists, U Po Kyo and U Po Hlaing.

Having repaired, restored and consecrated the Main Stupa and the Matha-Kuar Temple, Ven. Chandramani turned his attention to education. In 1929, he established a Free Primary School at Kushinagar. It was followed by the Buddha High School in 1934 which was later upgraded to an Inter College, and then further upgraded to Degree College. In 1936, he established the Mahaparinirvana Sanskrit Paathshala which is now functioning at Kasia. In 1944, Ven. Chandramani established the Mahavir Junior School at Kushinagar. All these institutions have turned Kushinagar into a worthy seat of learning, and brought education within easy reach of the people of the nearby villages.

Ven. Chandramani was a great saint and scholar. He inspired many Indians and foreigners to seek refuge in the Buddha Dhamma. Amongst the Buddhist monks ordained by him were: Venerables Achhutananda, Amritananda, Dharmarakshita, Jinananda, Satyananda, Sangharakshita, Vijayananda, Vishudhananda and others. Finally, Ven. U Chandramani had the proud privilege of being the Dhamma-Guru of Dr. B.R. Ambedkar who embraced Buddhism at his hands on 14 October 1956 at Nagpur, and brought millions of his followers to the fold Buddhism.

Ven. U Chandramani Maha Thera passed away at Kushinagar on 8 May 1972, at the ripe age of 96, after more than seventy years' meritorious service to the cause of Buddhism in India.

9

VEN. FUJII GURUJI

The Most Venerable Nichidatsu Fujii, popularly known as Fujii Guruji, was born on 6 August 1885 in a peasant family of Sakanashi, village situated in the Great Outer Crater of Mount Asso in Kyushu, one of the four major islands of Japan. He had his primary education in the village school and then joined the higher Agricultural Institute at Usuki. It was here that he was attracted by the teachings of Saint Nichire'n (1222-1282) who believed in the supermacy of The Lotus Sutra. In March 1903, he renounced the worldly comforts and was ordained as a novice Samanera by Ven. Nichiei Adachi, the Chief Abbot of the Hoonji Temple of the Nichiren Sect in Usuki. He was then 19 years of age. For the next 14 years, he practised extreme ascetic practices and made an in-depth study of Buddhism under various learned teachers. In 1917, at the age of 33, Fujii Guruji began propagating the teachings of the Buddha, or the task of enlightening people as he calls it He began his mission with Korea. His usual mode of preaching was beating the drum and chanting all the while 'Namu-Myho-Renge-Kyo' which means 'I devote myself to the Sutra of the Lotus of the Wonderful Law'. From Korea, he went to China. His curious method of religious preaching was often objected to or ridiculed by some people but he continued the practice undeterred wherever he went. Returning to Japan in 1924, Fujii Guruji founded the first monastery of the Japan Buddha Sangha in Fuji district.

St. Nichiren had predicted that the Buddhism of Japan would without fail return to India. Inspired by this prediction, Fujii Guruji thought of propagating the doctrine in India, and accordingly set out on his mission in 1930 via Manchuria, Hongkong and

---

1. *Nichi* means the sun, which eliminates darkness, and *ren* means the lotus which brings forth a pure white blossom from the mire of the swamp.

Singapore reaching Calcutta in January 1931. Not finding any foothold in Calcutta, he went to Bombay and began staying in the neighbourhood of a Japanese cemetery with the help of a Japanese family living nearby. In Bombay, Fujii Guruji just walked around the town, beating the drum and chanting the prayer, but engaged in no particular missionary work. Some children of the colony near the cemetery came to his hut out of curiousity and also learnt to chant the prayer 'Namu-Myho-Renge-Kyo'. In February 1933, he went to Sri Lanka and climbed Mt. Sripada. Returning from Sri Lanka in September 1933, Fujii Guruji went to see Gandhiji and met him at Wardha on October 4. Gandhiji was so overwhelmed by the solemn chanting of the Mantra-Nomu-mhyo-ho-ren-ge kyo—that he gave it a pride of place in the prayer in his ashram.

Two years later, in 1935, Fujii Guruji again went to Calcutta and built a small Buddhist temple there. In 1936, he set about propagating the faith in Rajgir in Bihar, the place where the Buddha is believed to have delivered the Saddharma-Pundarika (the Lotus Sutra) on the Vulture Peak, Gijjhakuta (Gridharkuta). He writes in his autobiography : "Every morning I went up Gijjhakuta before dawn to pray and to watch the sunrise. At that time there was not even a footpath on the mountain, and I had to walk my way through bushes from which anything might suddenly emerge. Yet, it was my vow to set the first foothold of Buddhist revival in India on Gijjhakuta in Rajgir, and I could not alter it. It became my daily routine, while staying in Rajgir, to go up Gijjhakuta before daylight and watch the sunrise". (My Non Violence, P. 97).

Inspired by the missionary zeal of Fujii Guruji, one of his disciples, Tenjo Watanbe, came to India in 1936 and began assisting him in the Dhamma work. When the Second World War broke out, Fujii Guruji went back to Japan in March 1938. Ven. Tenjo Watanbe stayed back to supervise the construction of the Japanese Buddhist Temple at Worli, Bombay. The temple was nearing completion when Ven. Watanbe was detained in 1940 by the British Government ; and later repatriated to Japan Consequently, the Nipponzan Myohoji Temple at Worli, which was financed by the Birla Brothers, was formally inaugurated only in 1956.

As part of the 2500th Buddha Jayanti Celebrations, an International Buddhist Conference was organised by the Government of India in New Delhi in November 1956. Fujii Guruji also participated in this Conference. He records that at this Conference, Jawaharlal Nehru, the Prime Minister of India, suddenly proposed a specific reconstruction programme for Rajgir as he felt that, unlike some other Buddhist shrines, there was nothing at Rajgir for the pilgrims and tourists to see. Hence, a Rajgir Reconstruction Committee headed by Nehru himself was constituted. Four other members of this Committee were: Finance Minister, Morarji Desai; Chief Minister of Bihar; former Governor of Punjab and former Ambassador to Japan, C.P.N. Sinha; and Fujii Guruji. Before any concrete progress could be made by the Committee, Nehru died in 1964. Consequently, former Finance Minister and then Deputy Prime Minister, Morarji Desai became Chairman of the Committee.

Fujii Guruji further records that as part of the Reconstruction programme, he offered to erect a stupa at Rajgir, and ultimately selected the Ratnagiri hill-top, which was more spacious than Gijjhakuta, hence a more suitable site for the stupa. This proposal was agreed to by the Reconstruction Committee as well as by the Archaeological Survey of India. After making necessary arrangements, the foundation stone of the Stupa or the World Peace Pagoda, as it is now known, was laid on 15 March 1965 by Dr. S. Radhakrishnan, the President of India. The actual construction of the Peace Pagoda began in 1968. What a difficult task it was to construct the Stupa atop the Ratnagiri hill can better be judged from what Guruji tells us. He says:

"In carrying out the project, cement work accounted for an important proportion, and required a lot of water, gravel, cement and reinforcing rods. All materials had to be brought up from the foot of the mountain. There was not a descent road, the materials could not be carried by trucks. They eventually had to be brought up by human power. Furthermore, it was a three-mile trip uphill".

"For the first mile there were stone steps, allegedly built by King Bimbisara that could be used, but the rest of the trip had to be made through trackless bushes. The government was building roads here and there, but we could not wait until their opening. We took a straight course toward the mountain top, and climbed through bushes. To carry water, each of us brought a canful on top of his head. In the same way, only one or two large reinforcing rods could be carried. If they were small, three or four could be hauled at a time. As the trip was six miles back and forth, each man could make at most three round trips a day. We recruited helping hands from nearby, including labourers from Calcutta, and there were 800 of them during the peak period". (My Non Violence, pp. 106-7).

Artistically designed by Prof. Minoru Okoka of Japan, and the noted Indian artist, Upendra Maharathi, the 160 feet high, gold-topped Santi Stupa, almost double the dimensions of the Sanchi Stupa, cost more than Rupees twenty lakhs. On completion, it was inaugurated by V.V. Giri, the then President of India, on 25 October 1969. In the chamber of this Stupa, the sacred Relics of Lord Buddha, presented by India to Japan in 1952 were also enshrined. The World Peace Pagoda atop the Ratnagiri is now the greatest attraction for the pilgrims as well as the tourists visiting Rajgir. For going to the top of the Ratnagiri hill, an aerial chairlift has been installed.

Fujii Guruji also constructed at Rajgir, a magnificent Vihara known as Nipponzan Myohoji Temple, a model of the Veluvanarama sangharama (Bamboo Grove Monastery) donated by king Bimbisara, where the Buddha had often stayed while at Rajgir. Built in an area of 32,400 sq. ft. it is the biggest Vihara in modern India. The inaugural ceremony of this Temple was performed on 24 October 1981.

Another Peace Pagoda built by Fujii Guruji, founder President of the Japan Buddha Sangha, is atop the historic Dhauli hill, in Orissa, where Emperor Asoka, after witnessing the large scale massacre in the Kalinga war, had sought refuge in the Buddha-Dhamma. The Kalinga Peace Pagoda is situated in ideal surroundings on the top of the hillock of Dhauligiri at a distance of 15 Km from Bhubneshwar, the capital of modern Orissa. The Rock

Edict of Asoka, with a beautiful figure of an elephant skilfully carved out of solid rock atop, is just on the newly laid road to the top of the Dhaulagiri. The foundation stone of the Dhaulagiri Stupa was laid on 25 January 1971. Built with some financial assistance from the Government of Orissa, this Peace Pagoda was inaugurated on 8 November 1972. By now, over forty Peace Pagoda have been built by Fujii Guruji in Japan, India, Sri Lanka and Gr. Britain.

Ven. Fujii Guruji passed away in Japan at the ripe age of 100 years in January 1985.

10

VEN. MAHAVIRA

Venerable Mahavira or Mahavir Swami, as he was popularly known, was the first Hindu in modern times to become a Buddhist monk. Mahavira was nephew af Babu Kunwar Singh of Jagdishpur in Bihar under whose leadership he took part in India's first Revolt against the British rule in 1857. After the death of Babu Kunwar Singh in 1858, Mahavira took to wrestling, and while taking part in the wrestling matches, he went to Sri Lanka via Madras. While in Sri Lanka, he studied Pali and was attracted towards Buddhism. In 1890, he was ordained as a monk by Ven. Indrasabha Nayaka Thera. In 1891, Ven Mahavira returned to India by way of Burma, and came to Kusinara or Kushinagar, as the place is now called, the sacred spot in district Deoria of Uttar Pradesh, where the Buddha lying between the two Sal trees had attained Parinirvana in B.C. 483.

Kusinara came to light in modern times in 1861-62 when Sir Alexander Cunningham identified for the first time the Kasia ruins with the site of Buddha's Maha-parinirvana. Subsequently, in 1876 A.C.L. Carlleyle, Cunningham's assistant, carried out extensive excavations at the site, and completely exposed the Main Stupa and discovered right at its front, the famous Nirvana statue of the Buddha buried in the debris of the ruins of an oblong shrine. Carlleyle also discovered a statue of the Buddha. in the mound locally called Matha-Kuar. He also exposed the shrine to which this statue belonged.

Notwithstanding these discoveries of far reaching importance, Kusinara was a deserted place when Ven. Mahavira chose it for his permanent abode in 1891. After settling a little bit, he repaired the Nirvana, Temple, which had not been looked after properly by the Archaeological Survey of India since its initial repairs in 1876.

Encouraged by his presence. the Buddhist pilgrims, particularly from Burma. began to visit Kushinagar. Therefore, Ven. Mahavira purchased in 1898 a plot of land, and constructed thereon a Dharmashala in 1901 for the convenience of the pilgrims. The cost of the Dharmashala building was borne by a devout Burmese Buddhist, Maung Khee Zarhee, also called Khezari Babu. and some other Burmese Buddhists. In 1902, Ven Mahavira constructed at Kushinagar a Buddha Vihara, which was, in fact, the first modern Vihara to be constructed any where in India. Thus engaged in this noble task of creating a base for Buddhist revival at Kushinagar, Ven. Mahavira passed away in March 1919.

11

VEN. KRIPASARAN

Venerable Kripasaran Maha Thera, the founder of the Bengal Buddhist Association, was born in a poor but pious Barua Buddhist family of Uninepura in the Chittagong district (now in Bangladesh) on 22 June 1865. His father died when Kripasaran was just ten years old. He had, therefore, to do odd manual labour as a boy to earn his living. Having been taught the virtues of Dhamma by his parents, he spent much of his spare time in the local Vihara. His quiet and calm nature, his reflective stance and meditative look soon attracted the attention of the Ven. Sudhan Chandra Maha Thera, the head of the Uninepura Vihara, and was ordained by him as Sramanera at the age of 16, on 1st of Vaisakha in 1881. Sometime after this, one of the pioneer Theravada monks, Ven. Puranachara, who had been trained in Ceylon, and was in fact one of the six Maha Theras who founded the renowned Ramana Nikaya of Ceylon, returned from Ceylon and settled at the Uninepura Vihara. Impressed by the talented and disciplined young Kripasaran, Ven. Purnachara ordained him as a full-fledged monk in 1885 and gave him the new name of 'Chandrajyoti'. But his parental name struck, and he was all along known as Kripasaran.

When in 1886 Ven. Purnachara decided to visit the sacred Buddhist shrines in India, he took Kripasaran with him. This pilgrimage widened the vision of Kripasaran. He resolved to dedicate his life for the revival of Buddhism in the land of its birth. Like Anagarika Dharmapala, he thought it appropriate to operate from Calcutta, the then Capital of India. At that time, there were a few hundred poor and illiterate Barua Buddhists, mostly from Chittagong, living in Calcutta for the sake of their livelihood. They had established a small Vihara in a rented building. Ven. Kripasaran made that Vihara the centre of his activities.

The primary object of Ven. Kripasaran was to organise the Barua Buddhists, the traditional Buddhists as we call them, and to reform the Dhamma being practised by them as due to ignorance they had become victims of corrupt practices. For giving shape to his ideas, he founded the Bengal Buddhist Association or the Baudha Dharmankur Sabha on 5 October 1892. Thereafter, he, with a begging bowl, travelled all over India, wherever Bengali Buddhists were living, soliciting funds for the construction of a Buddha Vihara in Calcutta. Eight years later, in 1900 A.D., he purchased a plot of land at 5, Lalit Mohan Das Lane (since renamed as Buddhist Temple Street), Kapilitola, Calcutta at a cost of Rupees 4500. Here, he constructed the Dharmankur Vihara in 1903, which became the headquarters of the Bengal Buddhist Association, and has been so ever since then. Same year, another Barua Buddhist monk, Gunalankara Maha Thera, came from Chittagong to Calcutta and started helping Ven. Kripasaran in his multifarious activities. Inspired by his activities, another Barua scholar, Swami Purnananda came forward to serve the Dhamma. He was ordained as sramanera in 1903. Two more to follow suit were : Nagendra (1906) and Kalikumar (1907). In 1908, Ven. Kripasaran founded 'Jagajjyoti', a Buddhist periodical in Bangla, under the editorship of Gunalankara Maha Thera and Swami Purnananda. This journal is now a bilingual quarterly in English and Bangla. In 1909, Ven. Kripasaran founded the Gunalankara Library which is now a Treasure House of rare books on Buddhism.

Ven. Kripasaran worked in close collaboration with Anagarika Dharmapala. Many eminent citizens of Calcutta also came forward to help him in his work. To name a few, Sir Ashutosh Mookerjee, Harinath Dey, Rai Bahdur Narendranath Sen, Editor of the 'Indian Mirror', Dr. Satish Chandra Vidyabhushan, Bhupendra Ghosh, Chunilal Bose and others were good friends of Ven. Kripasaran and often took part in the functions at the Dharmankur Vihara.

After consolidating his position in Calcutta, Ven. Kripasaran ventured out, and established a series of branches of the Bengal Buddhist Association at Simla (1907) Lucknow (1907), Dibrugarh (1908), Darjeeling (1910), Ranchi (1915), Shillong (1918) and Tatanagar, Jamshedpur (1922); thus creating awakening and a sense of kinship amongst the Bengali Buddhists living all over India. During his lifetime, Ven. Kripasaran also ordained a large number of Bikkhus. Besides those referred to earlier, his disciples included Bhikkhus : Bodhananda, Agrabamsa, Ananda, Aryalandar, Kajalkumar and Dharmadarsi. His life of devotion, dedication, self-denial and asceticism was an inspiring ideal for many more.

The Dhamma-duta work took Ven. Kripasaran in 1908 to Burma where he was invited by Ven. U Sagar Maha Thera and Tejabanta Maha Thera. Wherever he went, Mandalay, Moulmein and other places, he being a pious Buddhist from the land of the Buddha, was received with respect and reverence. In 1915, he visited Sri Lanka at the invitation of Anagarika Dharmapala. At Colombo, he was given a rousing reception by the Sri Lankan Buddhists. Thereafter, he toured the Island, visiting centres like Kalyani Chaitya, Anuradhapura, Mihinital, Kandy etc. and returned to India after spending six weeks there. These visits made him more firm in his resolve to work for the revival of Buddhism in India.

Besides religion, Ven. Kripasaran also took interest in spreading education. He got many high schools in Chittagong district affiliated to the Calcutta University, and also established new schools himself. In 1910, he convened at Calcutta a Convention of the Young Men's Buddhist Association in order to consider problems of the student community. He also organised a Buddhist Women's Conference in 1918 to focus attention on the problems of women. He was also instrumental in getting the Pali studies introduced at the Calcutta University. In pursuance of his efforts, the Government of India also agreed to sanction scholarships for higher studies in Pali in the U.K. Universities. The first student to be sent abroad under this scheme was Benimadhab Barua. He was the first Indian Buddhist to obtain D. Litt. from the Oxford University in 1917.

The last great act of Ven. Kripasaran was the convening of World Buddhist Conference from 6—14 December 1924 at Nalanda Park, Calcutta. At this Conference, assembled all the eminent Barua Buddhist monks and religious leaders from India, Bangladesh and Burma and pondered over the ways and means to further strengthen the revival movement. Same year, he established a Seema in the Dharmankur Vihara for the ordination of monks. The Seema was consecrated according to the Vinaya rules by the Bhikkhus headed by Ven. Kripasaran and was dedicated to the Sangha on 12 December 1924. Soon after this, Dharmadarshi Sramanera was given the higher ordination at this holy spot by Ven. Kripasaran himself.

Ven. Kripasaran Maha Thera passed away on 30 April 1926 at Calcutta leaving behind a rich legacy of faith and devotion. The Dharmankur Vihara, established by him, is now a worthy centre of Buddhist thought and culture.

12

DHARMANANDA KOSAMBI

Dharmananda Kosambi, a great Pali scholar of modern India, was born in a Maharashtrian family of a remote village in Goa on 9 October 1876. He was the youngest in a family of five sisters and two brothers. There being no proper schooling arrangement in Goa at that time, he learnt some Marathi at home and read few books available in the village. One day, in 1897, he read Lord Buddha's life-sketch in the Marathi monthly for the children, named, 'Bal Bodh' published by Vinayak Kondadav Oka from Bombay. He was so much impressed by the sublime story of the Buddha that he immediately decided to make a thorough study of the Buddha-Dhamma. About this sudden awakening, Kosambi later wrote : "I felt that whatever may be the difficulties, obstructions in my way I must study the Buddha's Teachings, and if I am able to do so, I will consider that the purpose of my life has been fulfilled".

In order to understand Buddha's teachings, Dharmananda Kosambi first thought of learning Sanskrit. With this object in view, he left his home in December 1899 and came to Pune to begin his pursuit of Sanskrit and Buddhism. After studying Sanskrit for sometime at Pune, Dharmananda Kosambi came to Banaras (Varanasi), where he spent a year and a half in the company of renowned Sanskrit scholars. Not satisfied with the knowledge of mere Sanskrit language, Dharmananda Kosambi went to Nepal in search of Buddhism. Disappointed at what he saw at Kathmandu in Nepal, Kosambi came back and went to Buddha Gaya, the Seat of Buddha's Enlightenment. There a Buddhist monk advised him to go to Sri Lanka where he could see and experience the living Buddhism. Accordingly, he set off for Sri Lanka and reached Colombo in March 1902. Soon thereafter, he embraced Buddhism and was ordained as a monk ; thus becoming the second Hindu to don the robes of a Buddhist monk in modern times. In Sri Lanka Dharmananda Kosambi studied Pali and Buddhism under the Venerable Hikkaduwe Sumangala Maha Nayaka Thera, the founder Principal of the Vidyodaya Pirivena. now the Vidyodaya University, in Colombo. After his studies for about one year in Sri Lanka, Kosambi returned to India. He had thought of going to Kusinara, the site of Buddha's Maha Parinirvana, but had to stay in Madras as he had no money to meet the travel expenses beyond Madras While in Madras, he came in contact with Prof. P. Lakshmi Narasu and other Buddhists of South India. At Madras, he also met some students from Burma. They persuaded him to go to Burma, and also made arrangements for his passage to Rangoon. In Burma, Ven. Kosambi practised Buddhist meditation like a true yogin, before returning to India in 1904.

On return to India, Dharmananda Kosambi spent about two years in visiting the Buddhist shrines. As he was penniless, sometimes he had to beg for his food From Calcutta, he went to Bombay. From Bombay, he went to Ujjain, Gwaliar, Sarnath, and then to Kushinagar. From Kushinagar, he went to Sravasti (Sahet-Mahet), and then came to Buddha Gaya via Banaras. With the help of a Burmese Bhikkhu, whom he met at Buddha Gaya, Dharmananda Kosambi again went to Burma from where he returned to Calcutta in January 1906.

Dharmananda Kosambi for a while returned to family life, and was married. His only son, D.D. Kosambi, was born in 1907. But Kosambi was not basically a family man. His inquistive mind prompted him to say 'good-bye' again to his home and family, and devote all his might to the cause of Buddhism. He again donned the robes of a Buddhist monk and wore the same much of his life. Towards the end of 1906, he was asked to teach the newly developed Pali programme at the University of Calcutta. He also taught for sometime at the National College at Calcutta which was founded in the wake of the Swadeshi movement. He was, however, keen to preach the Buddha's message to his own people in the Marathi-speaking region. Therefore, when the Maharaja of Baroda, Sayajirao Gaekwad, invited Kosambi to come to Baroda and write books on Buddhism atleast for three years, he gladly consented and went to Baroda. Soon thereafter, with the help of Sir R.G. Bhandarkar, Kosambi persuaded the University of Bombay to introduce the study of Pali language at the University. He himself taught Pali from 1912-1918 at Fergusson College in Pune; thus establishing firmly the study of Pali in Devanagari script in India.

Dharmananda Kosambi also served in the National University of Gujarat started by Mahatma Gandhi. In the meanwhile, Kosambi also published a Pali Reader in 1914-16 with his student C.V. Rajwade, and some other texts.

On an invitation from Dr. James H. Woods of Harvard University, whom he had taught Pali in Bombay, Kosambi went to America in 1910 and worked for about two years with him on Buddhaghosha's Visuddhimagga. He again went to the States in 1918 and spent four years at Harvard University editing the Visuddhimagga. Kosambi again went twice to America finally completing the Devanagari edition of Visuddhimagga in 1927, and getting Ph. D. for the same from the Harvard University in 1929. He completed the English edition of the Visuddhimagga in 1932. The Devanagari edition of the Visuddhimagga was published by Bhartiya Vidya Bhavan, Bombay in 1940. The English edition of the Visuddhimagga was published by the Harvard University in 1950. Dharmananda Kosambi also made notable contributions in the field of Abhidhamma. His commentary on the Visuddhimagga, titled 'Dipika', and Devanagari edition of Abhidhammathasanghho (with commentary-Navanitatika) are of great help to the students of Abhidhamma.

While working for the cause of Buddhism, Dharmananda Kosambi was also associated with the freedom movement. He actively participated in the Non-Co-operation Movement in 1931 as a result of which he was imprisoned also.

Keen to spread Buddhism amongst the downtrodden classes, Dharmananda Kosambi built in 1937 a small Buddha Vihara at Parel, a mill workers area of Bombay, and called it 'Bahujana Vihara' or 'the Buddhist temple of the masses'. In order to popularise Buddhism, he also wrote a number of books in Marathi. His most popular book in Marathi 'Bhagwan Buddha' was published in 1940. This book has since been translated and published in Hindi, Assamese, Gujarati, Kannada, Malyalam, Oria, Sindhi, Tamil and Urdu by the Sahitya Akademi, New Delhi. And this was one of the books which profoundly influenced Dr. Ambedkar's approach to Buddhism. Some of the other important books written by Dharmananda Kosambi in Marathi are : Buddha-lilasara sangraha, Buddha Dharma ani Sangha, Samadhi-marga,

Jataka-Katha, Buddha-Sanghaca Paricaya, Hindi Sanskriti ani Ahimsa, and Marathi translation of Sutta-Nipata. Kosambi also wrote a few books in Gujarati while some others were translated into Gujarati. His books in Gujarati are: Buddha-lila sara sangraha, Buddhasangha na Paricaya, Samadhi-marga, Bhagwan Buddha na dharmasamved, and Buddha, Dharma ani Sangha.

As the Bahujana Vihara at Bombay did not function to the satisfaction of Dharmananda Kosambi, he handed it over to the Maha Bodhi Society of India for proper management. Later, he came to stay at Sarnath, and helped Pali scholars like Ven. Jagdish Kashyap. Having worked devotedly for the cause of Buddhism for over forty-five years, and having fulfilled his vow of knowing and preaching Buddha's Teachings, Dharmananda Kosambi passed away on 4 June 1947 at Gandhi's ashram in Sevagram.

13

VEN. BODHANANDA

Bhadant Bodhananda Mahasthavir was one of the most eminent Buddhist monks of modern India, and he played a very significant role in the Buddhist revival movement. He was born in 1874 in a Bengali family at Chunar (old Sunsmaragiri) in Mirzapur District, Uttar Pradesh. His parents passed away when he was just a child. So, Mukand Prakash. as he was then known came to live with his widow aunt who was residing at Varanasi. From childhood, he liked the company of Sadhus and Mahatmas. Influenced by the environments, he became a Sadhu and was given the name of 'Nij Bodhananda'.

In 1896, Bodhananda met per chance some Buddhist monks who were on a pilgrimage to Sarnath. He was impressed by their serenity, dignity and way of life, and was attr..cted to Buddhism. Ven. Bodhananda has written like this about his pilgrimage to Buddhism :

"In 1896, when I was busy in serving the 'famine affected' people in Kashi I luckily met some Buddhist monks from Ceylon. From them I came to know of Buddhism. On study I found that whatever good and of public well-being points are in modern Hinduism, they have all come from Buddhism. Buddhism is the original and Sanatan religion of India and it has the capacity of making India, especially Hindus, a well knit nation as there is no place for caste-system and in-equality in Buddhism. Hence I decided to preach and propagate the teachings of the Compassionate Buddha. From then onward I continued preaching Buddhism".

Bodhananda came to live permanently in Lucknow in 1904. As a Vaishnava Sadhu, he built the Mahavir Shanti Mandir in Ameenabad Park, Lucknow. He also installed an image of the Buddha in this temple. This was objected to by some Hindus. Thereupon, the indomitable Bodhananda, with the help and assistance of some friends, moved to the Risaldar Park area of

Lucknow. This was during 1907-1909. Not satisfied with the Hindu way of life, Bodhananda ultimately became a Buddhist monk on 4 October 1914 after taking Upasampada at the hands of Ven. Kripasaran Maha Thera and Ven. Gunalankar Maha Thera. After becoming a Bhikkhu. he retained his well-known name—Bodhananda. His ordination was in a way a major landmark in the Buddhist revival movement. He was the first Bhikkhu to be ordained in modern India. As at that time there was no consecrated Seema in India for the ordination of monks, Ven. Bodhananda was ordained in a boat in the river Ganges near Calcutta. (According to the Vinaya, a Bhikkhu can be ordained on water in the absence of a consecrated land Seema).

In 1916, Ven. Bodhananda founded the Indian Buddhist Society, with headquarters at Lucknow, in order to preach and propagate Buddhism in North India. In 1925 he constructed a beautiful Buddha Vihara at Risaldar Park, Lucknow. He also established a Buddhist Library to which he added a large number of books in Pali, Sanskrit, Bengali, Hindi, Urdu, Persian and English. With the establishment of this Vihara and the Library, Lucknow became a good centre of Buddhism. And over the years, Ven. Bodhananda inspired many persons, including Rahul Sankrityayan, to come to the religion of the Buddha.

Besides being affluent orator, Ven. Bodhananda was also a prolific writer. Three important books written by him in Hindi were "Bhagwan Gautama Buddha—Jivani aur Updesh", "Mul Bharatvasi aur Arya" and "Baudhcharya Padhiti". In addition, he wrote dozens of small pamphlets on religious and social aspects for wider circulation amongst the masses.

Ven. Bodhananda was a straight forward man of truthful nature. He was totally opposed to caste system and untouchability. He could not tolerate any body defending caste-system, which he considered the root cause of all the ills in the Indian Society, specially the cruel treatment meted out to the downtrodden. Therefore, to take care of the socio-economic needs of the people, he founded in 1928 'Nava Ratana Samiti' which later came to be known as the 'Backward Classes League'.

Ven. Bodhananda passed away, at the ripe age of 78, on 11 May 19͜2 leaving behind a fertile field for Buddhist revival in Uttar Pradesh. As per his "Will", the Buddha Vihara complex built by him was later on taken over by the Maha Bodhi Society of India.

14

RAHUL SANKRITYAYAN

Mahapandit Rahul Sankrityayan, a prominent Buddhist scholar and creative Hindi writer, was born as Kedarnath on 9 April 1893. His father, Goverdhan Pande, of village Kanaila in Azamgarh district, Uttar Pradesh, was a farmer of modest means. He was married to Kulwanti Devi, the only daughter of Ramesharan Pathak, of village Pandaha in the same district, situated at a distance of about ten miles from Kanaila. Kulwanti used to stay with her parents at Pandaha, where Kedarnath was born. His maternal grand-father, an ex-serviceman, was very fond of Kedar and wanted to give him the best of education. So at the age of five, Kedar was sent by him to the nearby Primary School at 'Rani Ki Sarai'. He was very good at studies and used to complete the course much earlier than other boys. To quote his own words: "Reading was not at all difficult for me. In fact, for the studies which I could complete in four months, unnecessarily twelve months of mine were being wasted". Though so good at studies, yet Kedarnath had no interest in the studies.

While studying Urdu in the primary school, the following couplet by Navzinda Bajinda caught his imagination :

> Sair kar duniya ki gafil zindgani phir kahan
> Zindgani gar kuchh rahi to naujavani phir kahan
> (Oh you ignorant and idle, go and travel all over the wide world. You are not going to have another life for this. Even if you live longer, this youth is not going to return.)

Rahul Sanskrityayan quotes this couplet several times in his autobiography. Inspired by this philosophy of 'seeing the world' and his rebellious and adventurous nature, prompted Rahul to run away from home when he was just 13 years old and had only passed the sixth standard. So in 1907, he left his home with just Rs. 22 in his pocket and headed for Calcutta. There he met some other youngsters like him and stayed with them. But they could not sustain for long for lack of employment. Hence, after four months stay in Calcutta, he returned to village, and resumed his studies. But he still dreamed of 'seeing' the world. And he again disappeared from his home. This time he was lucky to get a job as an Assistant at a famous tobbacco shop in Calcutta. Here on eating some intoxicating sweets, he fell seriously ill and had to be hospitalised. On recovery, he returned to his village Kanaila.

While his employers were urging him to return to Calcutta, Rahul's mind was working in another direction. He wanted to learn Sanskrit, and to lead the life of a mendicant. With this resolve in mind. he took to the road again, and went on foot to Ayodhya, and Moradabad. As he had no money, he travelled without ticket to Hardwar. From there, he travelled in the company of some wandering sadhus to Rishikesh, Devaprayag, Badrinath, Kedarnath, Jamnotri and Gangotri. Finally he, along with his classmate Yogesh, returned to Varanasi in October 1910, where he lived in the ashram of Chakrapani Brahmachari and started learning Sanskrit. There he even tried to get the blessings of some gods and goddesses by undergoing difficult siddhis and namajap. But when for eight days no god or goddess gave him 'darshan' he felt so much disappointed and distressed that he consumed some poisonous fruit which nearly killed him. This shattered Rahul's blind faith in the gods and goddesses. In the meantime, he also came into contact with Pandit Ramavatar Sharma, who was a great scholar and rationalist. Encouraged by him, he took admission in the seventh class in the Dayanand School at Varanasi, where he learnt English. But formal education eluded him again.

About this time Mahant Lakshman Das who had his math at Parasa in district Chhapra, Bihar, came to Banaras in search of a disciple. He saw Rahul, and asked him to accompany him to Parasa. Rahul agreed to the proposal thinking that by becoming a Sanyasi he might be able to continue his studies, and also say 'goodbye' once for all to his home. Accordingly, in September 1912, he went to Parasa where he was given initiation by the Vaishnava Mahant by reciting some mantras and also stamping his body by a hot brass rod. His name was also changed from Kedarnath to Ram Udar Das. At Parasa, the life was comfortable, enough to eat but there was practically no scope for him to continue his studies So the 'hunger' of knowledge and 'lust' of travel prompted the rebellious Kadar, now Sadhu Ramodardas, to leave Parasa. Hence, once again, in July 1913, he took to the road. First he went to Hajipur. Then travelling via Asansol, and Kharagpur, he reached Puri. After seeing the Jaggannath temple at Puri, he went to Madras. As a sadhu, he toured the whole of South India visiting Punnamalai, Pachchaperumal, Tirumishi, Tinnaur, Tirupati, Tirukalikundam, Kanchipuram and Rameshwaram. At Tirumishi, he stayed for a long time and learnt the Tamil language.

After completing his visit to the South, he returned to Parasa in 1914 via Pune, Nasik, Ujjain, Ahmedabad, Bhopal, Allahabad and Varanasi. At the math, he again found the life stiffling and not conducive to his ways of free thinking and to the achievement of his ideal of acquiring more knowledge. So he again left Parasa secretly and went to Ayodhya. Here he came in contact with the Arya Samaji preachers and started studying the Vedas.

On coming to know of his whereabouts, his father came to Ayodhya and took Rahul home. But soon he disappeared again from Kanaila and went to Paryag (Allahabad) where a Kumbh mela was on. After the Kumbh fair was over, he tried to find some suitable job which might enable him to learn while earning. But in vain. Then he came to know that at Agra there was an Arya Samaj institute where education as well as boarding was provided free. Accordingly, he went to Agra and joined the Arya Musafir Vidyalaya in January 1915. For two years, he learnt Sanskrit, Arabic, and theology of various religions. He improved upon his knowledge of English as well. The changed environments influenced him so much that Ramodardas again started writing himself as Kedarnath Vidyarthi.

After completing the two year course at Agra, he went to Lahore and took admission in the Sanskrit Department of the D.A.V. College. At that time, Lahore was the stronghold of the Arya Samaj movement. Rahul was also enrolled as an Arya Samaj activist. In 1916, he was deputed to visit the Arya Samaj centres in U.P. While he was at Ahraura (Mirzapur), his father came once again in search of him, and pressed him to return home. But Rahul was adamant. He even tried to run away from Ahraura. His heart-broken father managed to catch him at the railway station, and accompanied him upto Banaras. On the way, Rahul impressed upon his father not to stand in his way as he was determined to follow the path already chosen by him. His father, Goverdhan Pande, last of all realized the futility of taming the rebellious son, and with a heavy heart, took leave of him. This was the last meeting of father and son. While parting, Rahul took a vow not to enter the Azamgarh district till he had reached the age of fifty years.

Rahul Sankrityayan was soon disillusioned with the Arya Samaj also as he found that the Arya Samaj tenets were dogmatic and a blind alley in many respects. Then a chance meeting in 1917 with Ven. Bodhananda at Lucknow proved a turning point in his life. He writes :

"First of all, I heard of the Buddha in 1910. Towards the middle of that year, after completing my first tour in search of knowledge, I came from Badrinath to Bareily where in the Dharmashala I came across Sadhu Khunnilal Shastri. He gave me a small pamphlet on Buddhism written in Sanskrit language. That meeting only slightly stirred my conscience. Next year, when I was going from my native village to Banaras I saw some Burmese Bhikkhus praying at Sarnath. Not knowing each other's language we could not communicate By saying Cakkhu Cakkhu, they made an attempt to explain but I could not understand much. Later on, I came to know that Cakkhu' is the Pali version of 'Chakshu' and what they meant to say was that 'Buddha is the eye of the world'. There after, when I was attracted by the Arya Samaj, I heard a few words about the teachings of the Buddha. This aroused my further curiousity towards Buddhism Since at that time there were no Hindi books on Buddhism, the only way to know Buddha Dhamma was to meet and talk to someone who may be knowing these teachings. Such a chance I got for the first time in 1917 when as a young Arya Samaj activist I went to Lucknow and stayed in the Arya Samaj there. There some one told me the name of a Buddhist monk, and the same evening I went to meet that Bhikkhu. This Bhikkhu was Bhadant Bodhananda Mahasthavir. He talked to me for a long time on various aspects of Buddhism and also answered my questions. At that time, there were many Arya Samaji scholars who in the guise of Swami Dayanand's theory of 'Guna-Karma-Sabhav' were still staunch supporters of the Brahmanical caste-theory based on birth. But in 1917 I was completely Nastik and fundamentally opposed to caste-system on any account and in any form. On talking to Bodhananda, I not only found confirmation of my own views but also learnt much about Buddhism which appealed to me".

In 1919, Rahul Sankrityayan appeared in the Sanskrit Shastri examination in Lahore but he failed. Then he went to Chitrakut and appeared in Kashi Nyayamadhyama examination in Sanskrit, in which also he failed. He, however, passed in first class in the Mimansa examination of Calcutta for which he had appeared at Jabalpur. Once again 'travel' captivated his mind. This time he was keen to see the Buddhist shrines as, after his meeting with Ven. Bodhananda at Lucknow, he had begun studying Buddhism and was attracted by the sublime and rational doctrine of the Buddha. In 1920, at the age of 27, he for the first time visited Lumbini, where the Buddha was born ; Bodh Gaya, where he had attained Enlightenment ; Sarnath, where he had delivered First Sermon ; and Kushinara, where the Buddha had attained Parinirvana. He also visited other Buddhist historical places like Rajgir, Nalanda and Sravasti. In his autobiography, Rahul Sankrityayan describes his visit to these shrines in an emotional and poetic language.

In 1921, the Indian National Congress launched the Non-Cooperation movement against the British rulers. Rahul Sankrityayan also took active part in this movement. He was arrested for his political speeches on 31 January, 1921 and was later jailed for six months. Thus the next six months, from February to August 1922, he spent in the Buxar jail in Bihar. On his release from the Jail, he was elected as Secretary of the Chhapra District Congress Committee. His close association with the Buddhist activities also began in 1922. At the Gaya session of the Congress held in December 1922, he forcefully pleaded with the Congress High Command to transfer the possession of the Maha Bodhi Temple to the Buddhists. its rightful owners. He was, however, greatly disappointed with the half-hearted approach in the matter by the Congress leaders.

Rahul Sankrityayan visited Nepal in the months of March-April 1923. Here he came in contact with some Buddhist scholars and monks from Mongolia and China. On return from Nepal, he was re-arrested for a political speech in Nepal wherein he had compared the role of 'blood' in freedom struggle to that of 'Chandan' in Puja. Consequently, he spent two years, from April 1923 to April 1925 in the Hazaribagh Jail. This two year period of solitary confinement was fully utilised by him in reading and writing. He had, in Sinhalese script, a copy of the Majjhima Nikaya in Pali which he reverently read daily. He translated four English novels into Hindi He also learnt French during this period.

In 1926, he undertook another hazardous journey. This time he went to Ladakh. He went via Punjab to Kashmir and crossing the Zozila pass to Leh. He traversed the length and breadth of Ladakh visiting various ancient monasteries. He returned via Lahul-Spiti-Kinnaur to Simla. And in the same year, he met at Meerut Harnamdas alias Brahmachari Vishvanath, a Punjabi youth. From their very first meeting, both became intimate life-long friends.

When the Vidyalankara Pirivena in Ceylon was in need of a Sanskrit scholar for teaching Sanskrit in that institution, Ven. Sirinivasa Nayaka Thera and D. Valisinha of the Maha Bodhi Society of India recommended Rahul Sankrityayan then known as Baba Ramodardas. So he joined the Vidyalankara Pirivena on 16 May, 1927 as teacher of Sanskrit. By now, he had acquired good knowledge of Hindi, Sanskrit. Urdu, Arabic, Persian, Tamil, Kannada, English and French. Now he turned his attention to Pali, and in a short time he not only attained proficiency in the language but also mastered the entire Pali Tripitaka and was awarded the highest degree of Tripitakacharya. During his stay in Sri Lanka from May 1927 to December 1928, he also studied many other Buddhist texts. He even learnt Sinhalese, and wrote a book in Hindi on Sri Lanka. He also wrote a commentary in Sanskrit on Abhidharmakosa, the famous work of Vasubandhu.

Towards the end of 1927, he asked Brahmachari Vishvanath to come to Sri Lanka. So the latter joined him there, and on February 10, 1928 he became a Buddhist monk with the new name of Bhadant Anand Kausalyayan. Ramodardas still continued to be a Hindu Sadhu. Of course, he had discarded his 'sadhu dress' and donned the ususal 'dhoti-kurta'. While still in Sri Lanka, he felt an urge to go to Tibet in search of the Buddhist sacred books which had been taken there by the fleeing monks from India who had to run for their life when the Muslim fanatics in the closing years of the 12th century attacked and razed to the ground the Universities of Nalanda and Vikramasila in Bihar. So early in 1929 Rahul Sankrityayan secretly entered Tibet via Nepal. On the Nepal-Tibet border, a Mongolian monk, Lobjad Sherav, whom he had met in Bodhgaya helped him to get the entry permit.

Trekking slowly on foot, sometimes on ponyback, on the hazardous and dacoit infested route, he last of all reached Lhasa on July, 19, 1929, passing through Shekar, Lharche, Narthang and Shigarche. At Lhasa, he was welcomed by Dharma Sahu's sons. He was the guest of Dharma Sahu in Kathmandu, Nepal and had carried letters for his two sons living in Lhasa. On reaching Lhasa, the capital of Tibet, he thought of presenting himself as a Buddhist devotee to the Dalai Lama. So he composed 151 stanzas in Sanskrit got them translated in Bhot and wrote them in a beautiful hand, and sent the poem through a confident of the Dalai Lama. The Dalai Lama was very much pleased and promised to invite him sometime later. But this meeting never took place. In the meantime, Rahul Sankrityayan went to Depung Gompa where he saw seven thousand monks living in various khamjans or dormitories for nationals of different countries. But there was no dormitory for Indians nor there were any Indian monks. Here he collected 16000 Bhot words, on small chits, and noted their translation in Nepali and Sanskrit. He also went to the oldest monastery in Samye where the body of Bhikshu Shanktarakshita was preserved. This temple-monastery was in ruins. So was the place where Indian scholars lived in the eleventh century and translated Sanskrit texts into Tibetan. Once it had a largest library containing rare books but the same had been destroyed in a fire long ago. Hence, he could not get even a single Sanskrit text. However, he bought a few manuscripts and paintings in Tibetan. He had planned to stay in Tibet for three years. But financial difficulties came in the way. When he needed some money for buying books, he wrote to Bhadant Anand Kausalyayan in Ceylon, who, with the kindness of Ven. Dhammananda and his dayakas, managed to send rupees three thousand to Tibet.

Having loaded on 22 mules the material collected by him-books, manuscripts, painting and thangkas, Rahul Sankrityayan accompanied by a Mongolian monk, Dharmakirti, left Lhasa for India on 24 April, 1930. On the way he purchased some more books at Shalu Vihar, Tasha Lhumpo and Narthang. After 39 days, the party reached Kalimpong. From there he came to Calcutta and then went to Sri Lanka reaching there on June 20. Besides Kanjur, consisting of the Vinaya and Sutras (108 volumes), and Tanjur consisting of various Abhidharma works (225 volumes), he brought as many as 1619 manuscripts in Tibetan and 150 paintings. All this valuable literary treasure was presented by him to the Patna Museum and is now preserved in its Kashiprasad Jayaswal Section.

On return from Tibet, Ramodardes decided to say 'good bye' to his Hindu garb. On 20 July, 1930, therefore, he donned the yellow robes of a Buddhist monk with the new name of Rahul Sankrityayan. As in the case of Bhadant Anand Kausalyayan, Ven. L. Dhammananda Maha Nayaka Thera was his Preceptor. From then onward, Rahul Sankrityayan began to devote his vast energies for the propagation of Buddhism by writing articles and books. His first book on Buddhism, namely, Buddha-charya, was published in 1930. He also began translating Pali works into Hindi language which at that time had no Buddhist literature worth the name. In July 1932, Rahul Sankrityayan and Bhadant Anand Kausalyayan went to London for Dhamma-duta work, on behalf of the Maha Bodhi Society. Rahul Sankrityayan came back within a few months via France and Germany while Anand Kausalyayan stayed in Europe for over twenty months. The year 1933 was spent by Rahul Sankrityayan in literary pursuit. Same year, another young seeker of truth, Jagdish Narain, met Rahul Sankrityayan at Patna. Next year, Jagdish Narain was on his way to Ceylon, where he embraced Buddhism and became a Bhikkhu at the hands of Ven. Dhammananda Maha Nayaka Thera, the Head of the Vidyalankara Pirivena, and assumed the name of Bhikkhu Jagdish Kashyap. This 'trio' of modern Buddhist monks (Anand, Rahul and Jagdish) from Punjab, U P. and Bihar played a major role in a variety of ways in the revival of Buddhism in India. Their first major contribution was to make available the Pali Texts in Hindi. The publication of these books was undertaken by the Maha Bodhi Society of India. Thus from 1933 onwards in quick succession, Dhammapada, Majjhima Nikaya, Vinaya Pitaka, Digha Nikaya, Samyutta Nikaya, Udana, Suttanipata, Jatakas and Milindpanha beeame available to the Hindi speaking masses.

Even such deep involvement in literary work could not damp Rahul Sankrityayan's eagerness for travel. So between 1934 and 1938, he went thrice to Tibet, and also to Japan, Korea, Manchuria, Soviet Russia and Iran. As a result of his three hazardous journeys to Tibet in 1930, 1934 and 1935, he brought back to India as many as 80 Sanskrit Buddhist works, some of which he himself edited and published. How hard Rahul Sankrityayan worked to discover and bring back to India these valuable books, which had not been available before, can better be judged by his experience at the Sa-Skya monastery during his third visit. He says :

"For me Sa-Skya monastery and its branches are most important as almost all Sanskrit palm-leaf manuscripts are found there. Permission was easily granted and on the third day after my arrival I received the manusctipts for copying. After finishing the fourth chapter of Vartikalankara I went to see the present hierarch—the head of Phunchhog palace. He insisted that I should see the Chhagpe Lakhang (the Manuscripts Library) of Lakhang-Chhenmo, as he had heard about the existence of Sanskrit manuscripts there. When I inquired from some other people the prospect appeared not very hopeful, but still I decided to go and see. With the permission of the Dolma palace authorities the seal was broken and little room on the roof of Lakhang-Chhenmo was opened, when a thin cloud of dust arose. We entered the room. The whole floor was covered with half an inch of dust. It seemed that the room had not been opened for fifty years. On the top of the book-shelf we saw bird-eggs. After clearing our throats which were getting choked up by the dust, we began to look around. On the wooden frames fixed on three sides of the wall thousands of manuscripts were kept. Very few of them were numbered. Some of them in appearance and size looked like Sanskrit palm-leaf manuscripts. After trying several times we felt disappointed, but very soon our hearts were brightened up when on the rack on the left side among the Tibetan manuscripts we found, one after another, many Sanskrit palm-leaf manuscripts. There were 25 bundles of them covered with two wooden boards and bound with very old worn-out leather ropes. After making a cursory investigation we found that there was a complete manuscript of the Pramanavartikabhashya, a sub-commentary of the first chapter of Pramanavartika and a complete copy of Asanga's Yogacara Bhumi.

With heart full of joy we took the two with us in order to copy them and from 26 May to 6 July my whole time was occupied in this work".

Being a rationalist and a free thinker, Rahul Sankrityayan was also attracted by Marxism. Inspired by the Russian Revolution of 1917, he wrote in 1922 a novel titled 'Baisvin Sadi' (Twenty second century) voicing his political views. He was also keen to visit Soviet Russia. At the earliest opportunity, therefore, in 1935 he visited Russia. He reached Moscow by train from Manchuria on 4 September and spent a fortnight in Russia. He was keen to meet Dr. Scherbatsky, author of the famous work 'Buddhist Logic.' But he was in Leningrad where Rahul Sankrityayan was not permitted to go. On 21 September 1935, therefore, Rahul Sankrityayan returned to India via Iran. He again visited Russia in 1937. This time he was invited by the Soviet Academy to teach Sanskrit at the Leningrad University. He stayed at Leningrad from 17 November 1937 to 13 January 1938. Here he met a young Russian lady, Lola (Ellena Narvertovna) who was Secretary of the Indo-Tibetan Department. She could speak French, English, Russian and Mongolian. Now she started learning Sanskrit from Rahul Sankrityayan and she taught him Russian. She fell in love with Rahul Sankrityayan, and persuaded him to marry her. Consequently, he discarded his robes of a Buddhist monk and reverted back to the status of simple Buddhist which he remained throughout his life.

On return from Russia in 1938, Rahul Sankrityayan became a political activist and threw himself fully in the Kisan-Peasant movement. He organised the Kisan satyagraha at Amavari and was jailed. He was released after a few months. In February 1940, he presided over the Kisan Sammelan held at Motihari. For his provocative speech there, he was re-arrested and spent the next 29 months in 1940-42 in Hazaribagh and Deoli jails. Rahul Sankrityayan devoted this entire period in enriching the Hindi literature. He wrote his monumental work 'Darshan-Dig Darshan' giving a critical exposition and Marxist interpretation of the Indian, European, Greek and Islamic philosophies. He also wrote a book titled 'Manav Samaj' in which he traced the progress of humanity through the ages. The third work written by him during this period was 'Volga se Ganga' a collection of twenty historical short stories. On release from jail, Rahul Sankrityayan travelled all over India during the years 1942-44.

During this period, besides five other books, he also wrote his autobiography (volume I) based on his diary which he used to maintain constantly. The second volume was published in 1950. And three more volumes were published posthumously. His autobiography is "a veritable treasure-house of information about anthropology, sociology, economic conditions, linguistic, travel hardships, geographical and geological matters, political pressures, archaeology and history of religion, obscure cults and belief patterns". An important happening of this period was his visit to his ancestral village. At the time of his last meeting with his father in 1916, he had taken a vow that he would not visit Azamgarh district till he had reached the age of fifty years. He kept the word. And in 1943, at the age of fifty, he fulfilled this vow by visiting his native village, Kanaila in Azamgarh district of Uttar Pradesh. By that time, both his father and mother had passed away.

In July 1945, the Russian Government invited Rahul Sankrityayan to the Soviet Union and appointed him as Professor in the Leningrad University. This appointment was as a sequel to the recommendation of Prof. Scherbatsky, the great Russian Indologist, who on his deathbed is stated to have said that "the only person who could succeed him to the Chair of Indology at the Leningrad University was Rahul Sankrityayan". From July 1945 to July 1947, therefere, he taught Hindi, Sanskrit, Tibetan and Buddhist logic at the Leningrad University. His wife Lola and son Igor were also with him in Leningrad. But as they were not permitted to accompany him to India, Rahul Sankrityayan came back alone and reached Bombay a few days after India had attained Independence on August 15, 1947.

From August 1947 onward, Rahulji primarily remained in India. In 1947-48, he was elected President of the All India Hindi Sahitya Sammelan, Allahabad. He was also nominated by the Government of India as a member of the Constitution Translation Committee. Alongwith this busy schedule, his own work of writing was also continuing. While engaged in the compilation of an Administrative Terms Dictionary, at his Masuri residence, Rahulji had some scholars to help him. They included Prabhakar Machwe, Vidyaniwas Mitra and Sengupta. Kumari Kamla Periar, a Nepali lady, used to type. Rahul Sankrityayan married her in 1950.

While staying at Masuri, Rahul Sankrityayan also wrote another monumental work 'Madhya Asia ka Ithas' which was dictated by him just in four months. Published in two volumes, it runs into about 2000 pages. This work earned him Sahitya Akademi Award in 1958.

Rahul Sankrityayan was a giant intellectual and scholar. He was a great creative Hindi writer. He was also a great linguist. He was well conversant with many Indian and foreign languages. Besides Hindi, he wrote in Sanskrit, Pali, Bhojpuri, Tibetan and English. Speed was one of his strong points. He is known to have written a pamphlet of about 30 foolscap pages in a day and a 500 page book in a month or so. He wrote novels, histories, scientific and philosophic books, travel records, biographies etc. He also translated many works and edited a number of Pali and Sanskrit works. In all, Rahul Sankrityayan has more than 150 books and pamphlets to his credit. His unpublished manuscripts include Pali Kavyadhara and Pali Sahitya ka Ithas. One marvels at his capacity to write under different conditions. "He never waited for the proper mood or cozy conditions. He wrote while on a train or a ship, at bus stops, in inns and chowltries, in camps, at home and in transit."

Prabhakar Machwe has listed 125 published works of Rahul Sankrityayan. Of these, sixteen are in Sanskrit, two in Bhojpuri and three in Tibetan. Those in Hindi are :

Literary

Autobiography (5 volumes), Biographies (16),Essays (7), Novels (9), Short Stories (4), and Travelogues (13).

Non-Literary

Compilation (3), Dictionaries (2), Folklore (1), History (5), History of Literature (2), Politics (8), Philosophy (3), Religion (8), Research (1), Science (1), Sociology (1), Translations (11), and Travelogues (8).

Out of these, the following books primarily relate to Buddhism : Buddha-Charya (1930), Dhammapada (1933), Majjhima Nikaya (1933), Vinaya Pitaka (1934), Digha Nikaya (1935), Tibet me Baudh Dharam (1935), Baudh Darshan (1942), Mahamanav Buddha (1956), and Baudh Sanskriti. A monograph on Sravasti was published posthumously in 1964. Among other books which substantially touch upon the Buddhist history and religion, mention may be made of his autobiography, his masterpiece historical fiction 'Volga se Ganga,' his philosophical monumental work 'Darshan-Dig-Darshan', and 'Atit se Vartman.' The travelogues written by Rahul Sankrityayan on his visits to Ladakh, Kinnaur (Kinner Desh), Sri Lanka, Tibet, China and Japan also provide a lot of information on Buddhism and Buddhist traditions.

The Sanskrit works on Buddhism edited and translated by Rahul Sankrityayan are : Abhidharma Kosh (1930), Vijnaptimatrata Siddhi (1934), Parmana-Vartika (1935), Adhyardha-Shataka (1935), Parmana-Vartika Bhashya (1936), Parmana-Vartika Vritti (1936), Parmana-Vartika Svavritti (1936), Parmana-Vartika Svavritti Tika (1937), Vigraha-Vyavartini, Vada-Nyaya, Vinaya Sutra (1943), Hetu Bindu (1944) Sambandha-Pariksha (1944), Nidana Sutra Pariksha (1951), Mahaparinirvana Sutra (1951).

As Rahul Sankrityayan was essentially a Buddhist scholar and writer, he never became an active preacher. Of course, he was keen for the revival of Buddhism in India. And when Dr. Ambedkar embraced Buddhism in October 1956, with half a millions of his followers, he welcomed the mass conversion movement and paid glowing tributes to Dr. Ambedkar. He expressed his views in this regard in a pamphlet titled 'Nav-deekshit Baudh' published in 1957 by the Buddha Vihara, Risaldar Park, Lucknow. He said that "there is no doubt that Babasaheb Ambedkar has done the greatest service to the country by initiating a mass Buddhist revival movement in India. History will never forget him for this unique role." He added that "Buddhism is not only necessary for the upliftment of the down-trodden people, its revival would also do a great good to the country as it would help in reviving the glory of the Buddhist sacred shrines which had hitherto been considered only as Museum pieces."

Rahul Sankrityayan, a self-taught multi-lingual scholar, had earned the highest degree in Pali studies from the Vidyalankara Pirivena in Sri Lanka in 1928. Later, he was honoured by the Vidyalankara University, Sri Lanka with the degree of D. Litt. (Hon.). For his services to the Hindi and Sanskrit languages he was honoured by the Kashi Pandit Sabha in 1939 by conferring on him the degree of Mahapandita. For the same reason, the Hindi Sahitya

Sammelan, Allahabad conferred on him the degree of Sahitya Vachaspati. He was also honoured by the Bhagalpur University, Bhagalpur with the degree of D. Litt. (Hon.). The Government of India also honoured him belatedly for his contribution to Indian literature by awarding him Padma Bhushan. By the time, however, the Nation honoured him, Rahul Sankrityayan had lost his memory and life had lost all meaning for him.

When in 1959, the Vidyalankara Pirivena was upgraded to the status of University, the new University invited Rahul Sankrityayan to head the Department of Philosophy. Accordingly, he took up his new assignment there in September 1959. While in Sri Lanka, he fell ill and returned to India in August 1961. In December 1961, his illness took a serious turn and he lost memory. He was taken to Russia for treatment but in vain. After seven months stay there, he was brought back to India. And on 14 April 1963, at the age of seventy, he breathed his last at his Darjelling house where a small memorial has been raised.

Rahul Sankrityayan will always be remembered for enriching the Hindi literature, and creating enormous Buddhist literature in Hindi when there was practically none. And his work "in bringing Tibetan manuscripts to light, editing many, commentary on, and translating some, was certainly one of the most long lasting of his contributions to world Buddhism".

15

BHADANT ANAND KAUSALYAYAN

Venerable Dr. Bhadant Anand Kausalyayan is well-known as a learned Buddhist saint and scholar. He is also famous as a creative Hindi writer. He was born on 5 January 1905 in a respectable Punjabi family in the village Sohana near Chandigarh. His father, Ramsaran Das, was a Headmaster in a High School at Ambala. Harnamdas, as he was named by the parents, and his younger brother Haridas, lost their father and mother in their childhood, and were looked after by their uncle.

After passing matriculation, Harnamdas joined the Freedom movement and suspended education. Later, however, when Lala Lajpat Rai established at Lahore a National College, he took admission in B.A. in that College. The newly established National College was in fact, a sojourn for the revolutionaries. Among his classmates were Shaheed Bhagat Singh, Sukhdev, and the famous Hindi writer, Yashpal. Being from a poor family, Harnamdas had to pass through hard days during his student life. In order to support himself, he used to sell Newspapers in the morning, and do some tuition work in the evening. During this period, he was also keeping indifferent health and often fell ill. Nevertheless, he passed B.A. examination with good marks at the age of 19 in 1924.

Two years later, his intution prompted Harnamdas to severe his ties, whatever little he had, with his kith and kin. He writes : "At the age of 21, I fell ill while staying at my cousin sister's house. Inspite of best medicines, the fever was persisting. Yet I wanted to run away from that place. But they were not willing to let me go in that state of health. So I made an excuse and told them that in a dream last night I took bath in the Ganga and found that my fever had disappeared. May be that if I take a Ganga bath, my fever may go. On hearing this, they reluctantly agreed to my going, and arranged a horse for my travel." He adds that aft er going a few miles, he sent back the horse, and himself went further and further into the wilderness of life.

While wandering hither and thither in search of inner peace, Harnamdas per chance met Rahul Sankrityayan (then known as Sadhu Ramodardas) at Meerut towards the end of 1926. Rahul Sankrityayan was at that time under the influence of Arya Samaj. Following his example, Harnamdas also became an Arya Samaji Parivarajik, and changed his name to Brahmachari Vishvanath. While parting, Rahul Sankrityayan advised Vishvanath to go round and visit the Buddhist shrines. This he did. Unlike the majority of the sadhus in those days, he was well educated, and was fond of reading books. One book which he always carried with him was 'Hero and Hero Worship.' He used to read this book whenever he could find time. On seeing this, some people used to remark in wonder, 'look, a thin and lean young Sadhu is reading an English book.' Soon Vishvanath got disillusioned with the Arya Samaj as its philosophy based on divine origin of the Vedas did not satisfy his keen intellect.

In December 1927, Vishvanath received a letter from Rahul Sankrityayan, who had earlier gone to Sri Lanka and was teaching Sanskrit at the Vidyalankara Pirivena, Kelaniya, asking him to come to Sri Lanka immediately. Accordingly Vishvanath set off for Sri Lanka via Madras-Dhanshakodi. On reaching Kelaniya, he started learning Pali, and was impressed by the Buddhist doctrine. He was ordained as a monk on 10 February 1928 by Venerable L. Dhammananda, Principal of the Vidyalankara Pirivena, and was given the new name 'Anand Kausalyayan.' About his conversion to Buddhism, he says: "The fact that Buddhism was not a revealed religion was appealing to him, and he found solace in the idea that Buddhist texts were not to be believed unquestioningly. The intellectual freedom of, and the depth of social commitment impressed him." He further adds that he had read Har Dayal's advice on choosing an occupation: 'Take the least, give most to society', and this influenced his decision to become a Buddhist Bhikkhu."

Bhikkhu Anand Kausalyayan studied Pali and Buddhism for 18 months devoting 18 hours a day under the able guidance of his Dhamma-Guru, and attained mastery over the Pali language and Pali scriptures. While studying Pali, he also translated 'Mahavamsa', a Pali chronicle of Sri Lanka, into Hindi. This was the first translation of Mahavamsa into Hindi.

In 1932, the Maha Bodhi Society requested Anand Kausalyayan and Rahul Sankrityayan to go for missionary work to London where Anagarika Dharmapala had opened a centre in 1928. Accordingly, the two learned Buddhist monks of India left for Dhammaduta work in London on 27 July 1932. While Rahul Sankrityayan returned to to India within a few months, Bhadant Anand Kausalyayan stayed back. He went to Liverpool, and later to Paris and gave useful talks on the Dhamma. He also went to Berlin and stayed there for some time in the Buddhistiche Haus founded by Professor Paul Dahlke. After useful Dhamma work in U.K., Paris and Berlin for over twenty months, he returned to Sri Lanka in 1934. For the next two years, he preached Dhamma in Sri Lanka. He traversed the length and breadth of the Island on foot. Wherever he went, he was enthusiastically welcomed by the people. They flocked in large numbers to hear Dhamma discourses from an Indian monk in their own Sinhalese language.

Bhadant Anand Kausalyayan and Rahul Sankrityayan were joined by Jagdish Kashyap in 1934. All the three pioneer Buddhist monks of Northern India were the product of the prestigious Dhamma institution, the Vidyalankara Pirivena (now a University) in Sri Lanka and had learnt the Dhamma lesson from the same Guru. They also became life-long friends, and worked in unison for the Buddhist revival in India. On return from Sri Lanka, the 'Trio' were together for some time in 1936 at Allahabad. There, it is said, that one day they expressed their individual programmes for the future like this : "Rahul Sankrityayan said that he would write as many books as possible ; Anand Kausalyayan said that he would love to undertake lecture tours and do journalistic work of writing articles, and serve the cause of Hindi literature. Jagdish Kashyap expressed his desire to spend his time in study, research and teaching, and in founding educational institutions".

True to his expressed wish, Anand Kausalyayan had all along been a Parivarajik, a wanderer, not sticking to any one place. In March 1939, the opening ceremony of the New Delhi Buddha Vihara, built by the Maha Bodhi Society, was performed by Mahatma Gandhi in the presence of a distinguished gathering.

Bhadant Anand Kausalyayan also attended this function. An old acquaitance of his was also present on this occasion. He recognised him and accosted him, after the opening ceremony was over, saying that 'why don't you go home these days'. Anandji replied, that 'he was not doing anything these days for which he need go there'. By now, 16 years had passed since Anand Kausalyayan had left his kith and kin. They were anxious to see him. On getting information about his presence in Delhi, his maternal uncle rushed from Punjab to Delhi. However, by the time he came, Anand Kausalyayan had gone to Sarnath. So his maternal uncle followed him to Sarnath, and ultimately saw there Harnamdas turned Anand Kausalyayan in the robes of a Buddhist monk.

For some time thereafter, Anand Kausalyayan stayed at Sarnath and edited Dharmaduta, the Hindi monthly published by the Maha Bodhi Society. About this time, Seth J.K. Birla had constructed a Dharmshala on the Maha Bodhi Society's land at Sarnath. To mark its opening ceremony, a yagya had been organised. Ven. Anand Kausalyayan objected to this un-Buddhistic ceremony. However, in deference to the wishes of Devapriya Valisinha, General Secretary of the Maha Bodhi Society of India, he promised not to give vent to his feelings in the public meeting. So early next morning, he left for Calcutta, and later expressed his views in an article titled 'Yeh hai Arya Dharam Sanghthan'.

Though born in Punjab, Bhadant Anand Kausalyayan loved Hindi and primarily wrote in Hindi. Of course, occasionally he also wrote in Punjabi, Urdu and English. In 1938, Gandhiji and other Congress leaders had established Rashtra Bhasha Prachar Samiti at Wardha (Maharashtra) in order to propagate the use of Hindi language in Non-Hindi speaking States. Later, Gandhiji favoured Hindustani and disassociated himself from the Samiti. Alongwith Gandhiji, Jawaharlal Nehru and Dr. Rajendra Prasad also resigned from the Samiti. At this critical juncture in 1941, Anand Kausalyayan, on the request of Purshottam Das Tandon took up the assignment of General Secretary of the Samiti. For the next ten years, he forcefully propagated the cause of Hindi through his writings and also devoted all his might to put the Prachar Samiti on a sound footing. He had practically started from scratch but within ten years he made the Samiti a well-established self-sufficient institution. When he resigned from the Samiti in 1951, the Rashtra Bhasha

Prachar Samiti had a large bullding complex, a large press, and about Rs. four lakhs in reserve. His work in the Samiti made him very popular with the Hindi lovers. In recognition of his services to Hindi, the Hindi Sahitya Sammelan, Allahabad, later honoured Bhadant Anand Kausalyayan with a degree of Sahitya Vachaspati.

During the period, he was General Secretary of the Rashtra Bhasha Prachar Samiti, Ven. Anand Kausalyayan wrote a number of books covering a vast field. The important books published by him during this period were: Buddh Vachan, Bhikshu Ke Pattar, Bhagwadgita ki Buddhiwadi Smeeksha; Tusli ke Teen Paat; Bahanebazi; Jo Na Bhool Saka; Kahan Kya Dekha; Jo Likhna Padha; Rail Ka Ticket. Besides these creative writings, he also published Hindi translations of the Pali books, namely, Mahavamsa (it was translated in Sri Lanka); Jataka (in six parts); Anguttara Nikaya (in four parts); Dhammapada; and Abhidhammatha Sanghho, Sacch-Sanghho.

In the following years, Ven. Anand Kausalyayan published some more works, such as, Pacheesvan Ghanta, Svantantr Chintan (translation), Dharm Ke Naam Par (translation), and Desh Ki Mitti Bulati Hai. During this period, he also travelled constantly between India, Burma, Sri Lanka, Japan, China and Nepal in connection with the Dhamma work before taking up the assignment as head of the Hindi Department, Vidyalankara University in Sri Lanka in 1959.

Bhadant Anand Kausalyayan was known to Dr. B.R. Ambedkar and had met him a number of times. These meetings became more frequent after 1951, and Babasaheb had even consulted him as to the modalities to be adopted at the conversion ceremony. However, on 14 October 1956 when the historic Conversion Ceremony took place at Nagpur, Ven. Kausalyayan was on a visit to China as leader of the Official Indian delegation in connection with the 2,500th Buddha Jayanti Celebrations in that country.

While on his way back to India, Anand Kausalyayan read in the aircraft, the news about the historic ceremony at Nagpur. Immediately on return, he went to Maharashtra and took part in a number of conversion ceremonies which followed the Great Ceremony at Nagpur. Dr. Ambedkar had planned another mass conversion ceremony at Bombay on 16 December, 1956. This was, however, not to be. He suddenly passed away in sleep at his Delhi residence on 6 December 1956. As the luck would have it, Bhadant Anand Kausalyayan happened to be on that day in Delhi. He accompanied Babasaheb's body to Bombay, and after performing the last rites, according to Buddhist tradition, on 7 December 1956, he gave deeksha to more than a hundred thousand people at the cremation grounds. From then onward, Maharashtra became his main field of activity. For more than a year in 1957-58, he extensively toured the country side of Maharashtra and guided the people on their new chosen path of Buddhism.

Before his sudden demise, Dr. Ambedkar had completed his monumental book on Buddhism and the same was in press. This book titled 'The Buddha and His Dhamma' came out in 1957. Immedinately on getting a copy of it, Ven. Anand Kausalyayan thought of translating the same into Hindi. While on a visit to Thailand he completed its translation during his stay in a Buddhist Temple in Bangkok. In the meanwhile, the ancient Vidyalankara Pirivena was upgraded and renamed as the Vidyalankara World University by the Govt. of Sri Lanka. The University invited three eminent Indian Buddhist scholars to head the three Departments, namely, Ven. Anand Kaysalyayan to head the Hindi Department; Mahapandit Rahul Sankrityayan to head the Department of Philosophy; and Dr. Shanti Bhikshu Shastri to head the Sanskrit Department. The new University started functioning on 17 June 1959. The first thing Ven. Anand Kausalyayan did in Sri Lanka was to prepare the footnotes indicating sources, not given in the original English edition of 'The Buddha and His Dhamma', and sent the Hindi manuscript to the People's Education Society, Siddharth College, Bombay for publishing the same. While in Sri Lanka, where he spent nearly nine years, he wrote a number of books, such as, Pali-Hindi Dictionary, Sri Lanka, Moggallana Vyakaran, Buddha Lankara, Sinhala Bhasha aur Sahitya, Anatamvada, Sanyojan-Das-Bhava Bandhan, and Baudh Dharm (Ek Buddhivadi Addhyan). During his sojourn in Sri Lanka, Bhadant Anand Kausalyayan used to come every year for two-three months to keep in touch with the Buddhist revival movement in India, and he invariably toured Punjab, Delhi, Uttar Pradesh and Maharashtra.

On return from Sri Lanka, after retirement from the Vidyalankara University in 1968, he thought of doing some concrete Dhamma work in Maharashtra where Buddhism had come to life overnight following the clarion call given by Dr. Ambedkar to his followers in 1956. The choice naturally fell on Deeksha Bhoomi, the sacred ground where Dr. Ambedkar on 14 October 1956 had, with half a million of his followers, taken refuge in the Buddha-Dhamma. Soon Bhikkhu Niwas, founded by him, at Deeksha Bhoomi became a centre of learning and training of young bhikkhus and lay leaders of Buddhism. In all, over hundred young men studied Buddhim under Ven. Anand Kaysalyayan's guidance Many of them have done post-graduate and Ph.D. Some of them have become Buddhist monks. Having seen hard days himself, Ven. Anand Kausalyayan was considerate and compassionate toward the students ·and helpful to every one who came to him with any problem. As for him, he had seldom been supported by any Buddhist organisation. His main stake for survival was the royalty from his writings. The first book to be published after his arrival at Deeksha Bhoomi in 1968 was 'Yade Baba Na Hotey', a biography of Dr. B.R. Ambedkar. It was followed by a series of books and pamphlets, namely, Kranti Ke Agardoot Bhagwan Buddh, Tathagata Ka Shashwat Sandesh, Bhagwan Buddh Ka Dharm, Baudh Gyan, Baudh Jeevan Padhiti, Rahul Sankrityayan, Baudh Dharam aur Marxwad, Bhagwadagita Tatha Dhammapada, Ram Kahani Ram Ki Zabani, Ramchrit Manis mein Brahminshahi Tatha Nari Ninda, Manu Smriti Jalai Gai Kyon, and Darshan (Philosophy). During the period under survey, Bhadant Anand Kausalyayan also published a book in English 'An Intelligent Man's Guide to Buddhism.' He also translated Dr. Ambedkar's monumental work 'The Buddha and His Dhamma' into Punjabi. This has been published by the People's Education Society, Siddharth College, Bombay.

For his services to Pali and Buddhist literature, Bhadant Anand Kausalyayan was honoured in 1971 with Vidyavaridhi, D. Litt. Degree by the Nava Nalanda Mahavihara, Nalanda.

Ven. Dr. Bhadant Anand Kausalyayan had to leave Deeksha Bhoomi in 1982 under compelling circumstances. His departure from there meant 'loss' of Deeksha Bhoomi and 'gain' of Buddha Bhoomi at Kampte, near Nagpur, where, last of all, the great

Parivarajik found his own nest. By now, a Buddhist Training Institute, a Bhikkhu Niwas and a Buddha Vihara have come up at Buddha Bhoomi which is spread in an area of eight and half acres donated by a noble Jhalla family of Nagpur. While thus engaged in the noble task of nourishing the Buddhist movement, through preachings and writings, Bhadant Anand Kausalyayan passed away at Nagpur, after brief illness, on 22 June 1988, at the ripe age of 83 years. His work at Buddha Bhoomi is now being carried on by his chief disciple, Ven. Dr. S. Medhankar.

Having been ordained in 1928, Bhadant Anand Kausalyayan served the Dhamma, as a Bhikkhu, for more than sixty years (1928-1988). He was closely associated with the neo-Buddhist movement since 1956. He spent the last 20 years of his life at Nagpur in the midst of the people of Maharashtra, and became their friend, philosopher and guide in all religious matters. In sum, Bhadant Anand Kausalyayan's contribution in sustaining the revival movement launched by Dr. Ambedkar surpasses all.

16

VEN. JAGDISH KASHYAP

Ven. Jagdish Kashyap Maha Thera was born as Jagdish Narain in 1908 at Ranchi in Bihar. But his ancestral home was in the village of Rounia in the district of Gaya. Rounia village is not far from the Barabar Hills in one direction and Rajgir and Nalanda in another. Jagdish Narain came from an old respectable middle class Hindu family. His father, Shyam Narain, was an employee in the Judge's Court at Ranchi. Since Shyam Narain was married to the only child of Ram Prasad of Ranchi, he was persuaded to work in Ranchi which became the second home of the former's family.

Jagdish Narain had his early school education at Ranchi. He passed his matriculation examination from Ranchi Zila School in 1925. Like all his brothers he was above average in his studies, but unlike them he was at once little rustic and simple in his habits, a bit unconventional and radical in outlook. He was sent to Patna for higher studies. He did his Intermediate Arts there from New College in 1927, and Bachelor of Arts from Patna College in 1929. From Patna he went to Varanasi and did his Master of Arts in Philosophy from Banaras Hindu University in 1931. In the following year he did a second M.A. privately in Sanskrit from the same University.

Already from school days Jagdish Narain had come under the influence of one of his maternal grandfathers, Ayodhya Prasad, an Arya Samaj Leader and preacher who had represented the Arya Samaj in USA. His academic training in Philosophy and Sanskrit helped him to take deeper interest in the Arya Samaj not only as an instrument of social change but also as a religious movement and a way of life. So, he joined one of the Gurukulas run by the Arya Samaj. He worked as the Principal of Sanskrit Vidyapith, the Gurukula at Baidyanathdham in Bihar during the year 1931-33. In this manner he got formally and intimately associated with the Arya Samaj.

As soon as he had passed his B.A. examination people had started coming to his parents with offers of marriage. But he decided to lead a celibate life and refused to be persuaded by his parents for marriage on the plea that if he did not marry he would be able to dedicate his life to the service of the country and society. He wanted to be ideally suitable for the Gurukula work.

The Gurukula years of Jagdish Narain proved to be a turning point in his life. On the one hand this was the period of his most intimate retationship with the Arya Samaj and its cause, but on the other hand, this was also period of his increasing interest in Buddhism. As the Principal of Gurukula, he was a strict disciplinarian and tried his best to guide the life pattern and duties of inmates in keeping with the ideals of the Arya Samaj and Vedic culture. He treated the inmates as one family (kula) and he participated in all activities of the young and the old for he was indeed a very energetic person and of strong physique. Gradually he became disenchanted with the organisation of the Gurukula and became very much concerned with the great gap between the precepts and the practice of the Arya Samaj, particularly as it related to the functioning of the caste system. He found that in Arya Samaj there were Brahmin Pandits, Vaisya Pandits, and Sudra Pandits, and the members of the Arya Samaj were not able to free themselves from their caste background in their social relationships.

After completing his M.A. studies Jagdish Narain wanted to do doctoral work in Buddhist Philosophy. Dr. Bhagwan Das, a respected citizen and philosopher of Kashi, as well as Ayodhya Prasad, his Arya Samaji Guru, encouraged him but also told him that in order to do so he must study Pali Tripitaka in original. While preparing for his M.A. examination in Sanskrit, Jagdish Narain had got his first introduction to Pali. At the Gurukula he continued his study of Pali. He was attracted by the very first verse of Dhammapada. It did not take him long to make up his mind to go to Sri Lanka for further study. He wrote an emotional letter in Sanskrit to the Vidyalankara Pirivena in Sri Lanka introducing himself as a young 'seeker of truth' from Magadha and expressing his desire to go there and study Pali in order to revive a lost tradition in India. Since he did not receive reply for a long time he gave up hope. But one day he received a letter from Germany written in

Hindi He was very excited to have it for this was the first letter he had got from a foreign country. This was from Rahul Sankrityayan advising him to see him during the latter's next visit to India. Jagdish Narain met him in Patna at the residence of K.P. Jayaswal, an eminent Indologist. Rahul Sankrityayan had brought there a vast collection of Tibetan manuscripts and crates were being opened one after another. Jagdish Narain stayed there for a few days and he was much impressed by the very sight of these manuscripts. Rahul and Jagdish, joined by ..P. Jayaswal, at times, discussed Buddha, Buddhism and Buddhist countries. One day Rahul Sankrityayan drew Jagdish Narain's attention to Buddha's teaching to the Kalamas in which the Buddha had asked not to accept what he said because he said it, but only after being convinced about it; and this made an impact on his mind. In his M.A. Philosophy course he had selected logic for his special papers and statements as above by the Buddha as well as the theory of Dependent Origination appealed to him very much. His interest in Buddhism increased beyond mere academic and he developed great respect for the Buddha. The Patna meeting thus further strengthened his inclination toward Buddhism and his desire to go to Sri Lanka. Rahul Sankrityayan and Anand Kausalyayan had already become Bhikkhus and had joined the Vidyalankara Pirivena. Through their good offices, Jagdish Narain was able to invite a teacher of Pali, Bhikkhu B. Seevali from Sri Lanka, and learnt more about Pali and Buddhism from him.

But when he told his parents of his plans to go to Sri Lanka, they were not prepared for this. They said with much feeling that they had reconciled themselves to his idea of not marrying for the sake of social work but they did not know how to accept the idea of his leaving the country. Finally, they had to give in at his repeated request and he left for Sri Lanka in November 1933 where he joined the Vidyalankara Pirivena.

In 1934 he was ordained into the Sangha by the Ven. L. Dhammananda Nayaka Mahathero of the Vidyalankara Pirivena. And Jagdish Narain became Bhikkhu Jagdish Kashyap, for Kashyap was not only his gotra but it was also a famous name in the history of Buddhism. Jagdish Kashyap now joined Rahul Sankrityayan and Anand Kausalyayan to make that 'trio' of the new Buddhist monks of northern India desitned to play a major role in a variety of ways for over four decades in the revival of Buddhism or what was perhaps more properly labelled according to them as the 'Buddhist Movement' of India.

During the period of his study and training in Sri Lanka, Bhikkhu Kashyap had started translating Dighanikaya into Hindi, jointly with Rahul Sanskrityayan. But the latter had planned a trip to Japan and he asked the former to accompany him. They sailed for Japan along with the manuscript from Calcutta. Though both got sick on board the ship, they continued doing their work. Their fellow passengers were amazed at their perseverence. When they reached Penang, the British Government police asked for Bhikkhu Kashyap and after questioning him for sometime showed him a telegram from the Government of India asking the local police not to permit him to proceed further. This happened on account of his participation in the non-cooperation movement of Mahatma Gandhi. So Rahul Sankrityayan and Kashyap had to part company there. The former proceeded to Japan and the latter stayed on in Penang. After having completed the translation work in Penang, Kashyap sent the manuscript to the printers in India.

The people in Penang were, in fact, happy at the conspiracy of circumstances that led to Kashyap's stay in Penang. Before proceeding to Japan, Rahul Sankrityayan had spent his time in Penang delivering speeches; he would deliver them in Sanskrit and Kashyap would translate them into English. People of Penang were very pleased with them for they were the first Indian Buddhist monks they had seen and they honoured them greatly. They arrangedto put up Bhikkhu Kashyap in a residence near the sea coast. He spent about a year in Penang. He chose to live in a Chinese monastery and learned some Chinese. A collection of his lectures at the Chinese Buddhist Association was published as a handy book under the title Buddha Dhamma in Penang in 1935. He also visited Singapore and other parts of Malayasia as well as Burma.

In Penang, due to contacts with some Chinese Mahayana monks he started practising meditation. He also practised psychotherapy and successfully cured some of his lay disciples of their ailments. So, when Bhikkhu Kashyap returned to Sri Lanka, he decided to spend sometime in a forest hermitage in order to practise more meditation. Rahul Sankrityayan did not like this new interest of Kashyap. He wanted him to go to London for Dhammaduta work and sent Anand Kausalyayan to dissuade him from practising Dhyana. But the young Bhikkhu Kashyap did not obey his two Guru bhais this time and spent a year in the Salagala forest. His stay in Sri Lanka and South East Asian countries thus provided him with an opportunity on the one hand for seeing Buddhism in practice and the working of the Sangha and its relationship with the laity, and on the other, for developing contacts with some leaders of Buddhism who were interested in its spread in India.

He returned to India toward the end of 1936. On his return, he went first to Allahabad and called on Rahul Sankrityayan at the residence of Pandit Udaya Narayan Tiwari and sought his forgiveness for not obeying his instructions to go to London. Rahul Sankrityayan smiled and patted him on the back; and Kashyap felt relieved. He spent some time there at Allahabad in the company of Rahul Sankrityayan, and of Anand Kausalyayan, who were living together. It is there that one day the 'Trio' outlined their individual programme for future Ven. Kashyap expressed his desire to spend his time in study, research and teaching, and in founding educational institutions. But before setting out on his mission, he went to Ranchi to see his parents as well as his eldest brother, to whom he was very much indebted for constant support and encouragement. The family and the neighbours saw him now in the yellow robe for the first time. He was received with mixed feelings. They also felt an element of pride and religious satisfaction. He told them about his plans to settle down at Sarnath and devote his time in the cause of Buddhism and Buddhist studies.

From 1937, his scene of activity moved to Sarnath. He became associated with the Maha Bodhi Society, and along with Rahul Sankrityayan and Anand Kausalyayan, the two other members of the 'Trio' started translating Pali Tripitaka into Hindi and doing other literary and scholarly works. But the entrepreneur in him was not satisfied with this only. He soon got involved in institutional organization and social service. With the erection of the Mulagandha Kuti Vihara, and because of the activities of the Maha Bodhi Society, the importance of Sarnath had increased both for the pilgrims and for the tourists. Devapriya Valisinha, the General Secretary of the Maha Bodhi Society, who had decided to found a High School at Sarnath, invited Ven. Kashyap to be the Head

Master. He agreed to head the institution on a very nominal salary just to comply with the official formalities. With his experience of formal education as well as of administration as Principal of the Gurukula he was able to put this new institution on a very stable basis. The school was first housed in the Birla Dharmashala. Bhikkhu Kashyap came thus in contact with Seth Jugal Kishore Birla, the well-known philanthropist of India who supported social, educational and religious activities of both Hindu and Buddhist organizations. As Ven. Kashyap did not want to house his school permanently in the rest house, he persuaded the Seth to donate land for the School. Leter, he went to Burma in 1939 and raised funds for its building. The school got financial stability and attracted students even from outside the locality.

While at Sarnath, he came in touch with Pandit Madan Mohan Malaviya and Dr. S. Radhakrishnan through the good offices of Seth Jugal Kishore Birla and succeeded in persuading the authorities of his alma mater, Banaras Hindu University, to start the teaching of Pali there. He offered his free services and accepted only Rs. 50 per month from Birla for his simple food and basic needs. He used to go daily to the University campus from Sarnath, a journey of 22 miles both ways. There was no bus service then. He used to cover the distance by a cycle rikshaw and would occasionally even walk the distance one way. Birla noted this and made a cottage for him in the University campus. This cottage known as Buddha Kuti has now been permanently assigned by the University authorities for use by teachers of Pali in the University. It was a small cottage of three rooms but was always over-crowded with students and monks from India and abroad who lived there along with him. Ven. Kashyap worked for nine years at the Banaras Hindu University. He not only taught Pali in the Department of Sanskrit but also Buddhist logic in the Department of Philosophy. He tried his best to introduce Pali and Buddhism in the graduate programme for M.A and Ph.D. degree and offered to teach all the papers single handed if the University failed to recruit an additional hand. But his proposal was not accepted then. The University has now the graduate programme and there are four teachers of Pali. During this period; the eminent doyen of Pali Studies, Dharmananda Kosambi had come to live at Sarnath, and later at Kashi Vidyapith in Varanasi. Bhikkhu

Kashyap took advantage of his presence and strengthened his knowledge of Abhidhamma and Visuddhimagga.

When India became independent in 1947, there was a new awakening and a sense of identity in the country. Bhikkhu Kashyap who hailed from Magadha and whose village home was close to Nalanda, had been thinking for long to revive the interest in Buddhism and in Buddhist studies in Bihar; to introduce the teaching of Pali (Magadhi) in the schools and colleges of Magadha and above all to re-establish the glory of Nalanda. He got an inner call that the time had come for a move towards that direction. First, he decided to create a climate for his projects in these areas. So in 1949 he set out for Magadha from Varanasi. He made a carika in Magadha in keeping with the ancient tradition of living on alms (pindapata). It was for the first time after eight centuries that the people in the interior villages of Magadha saw a Buddhist monk in yellow robes. And when Bhikkhu Kashyap spoke to them in their own dialect Magahi (modern Magadhi) it was indeed a pleasant surprise to them to know that he was one of them and that he belonged to their own area.

It was a long time since Buddhism had disappeared from most parts of India. In Magadha the people could still find the images of the Buddha scattered all over the land. But, with the exception of the students of history and archaeology, people did not know their identity and significance particularly in the country side. Even to this day images of Buddha and Bodhisattvas are worshipped under various names of Brahmanic and local deities. Bhikkhu Kashyap would remind them of the story of the Buddha and the history of Buddhism and impress upon them that it was their own thing. He would recite passages from the Pali Tipitaka to show how close was the language of Buddha to their own dialect Magahi and how it was their duty to revive the study of it. He also pointed out that the very name of the present state of Bihar was because the area was full of Viharas in ancient times. Often he would go to villages and identify modern place names with ancient ones, such as the modern village of Sari-Chak near Nalanda associated with the name of Sariputta. This whole story came as a kind of revelation to the people. Many listened to him with tears in their eyes.

Although he toured in various parts of Bihar (and even Northern Bengal) he concentrated mostly in Patna and Gaya districts, the old Magadha. He wanted to establish Universities both at Gaya and at Nalanda. He had succeeded in persuading the principals of the Gaya College, Gaya, and that of Nalanda College, which was located in Bihar-Sharif, to introduce the teaching of Pali in their institutions He offered to teach the subject himself in the latter without any payment. It became a popular subject, for the students found it easier than Sanskrit and it fetched more marks. He preferred Nalanda as the first place for his work. In the silent ruins of Nalanda he found at once a visible source of inspiration and challenge, and where the past seemed to beckon him strongly. Perhaps, being an educationist he found more of a cause in restoring the Nalanda University.

While Bhikkhu Kashyap was doing all this, the state government of Bihar was also planning to start three Institutes for the study of Sanskrit, Pali and Prakrit representing Brahmanic, Buddhist and Jain cultures, to all of which Bihar of ancient times had made very significant contributions. Mithila, Nalanda and Vaisali were selected respectively for the location of these three Institutes. J.C. Mathur, an I.C.S. Officer of the Bihar government, was primarily responsible for the establishment of these Institutes. Bhikkhu Kashyap was invited by him to organize the Institute of Pali at Nalanda. This was the founding of a new institution and everything had to be started from scratch. It demanded sacrifice and dedication. Nalanda was then a desolate place where no building was available even for temporary housing of the Pali Institute and so he started the work first at Rajgir and it was only later that he moved to Nalanda. This Institute developed into the present Nava Nalanda Mahavihara. He collected money locally and bought land and built small hutments to house the first staff and students, as well as a house which included his living place, a chaitya, and a meditation chamber in the basement, and a guest room. All this he made out of his own resources and donated to the Institute. He did much of the organizational and teaching work himself. It was all labour of love, a mission of life for him. Finally, he succeeded in persuading the Muslim landlord of Islampur who owned the land near the ruins of the old Nalanda University to donate sufficient land for the new building of the Nava Nalanda Mahavihara for housing the Institute. Dr. Rajendra Prasad, the first President of India, laid the foundation stone of the new building Nava Nalanda Mahavihara on 20 November, 1951. The newly founded Institute received on this occasion special messages of goodwill and gifts from the Buddhist countries. His Holiness the Dalai Lama sent a special representative with a completed set of Trbetan scriptures and an image of the Buddha. So also dedicatory presents and rare and valuable books were sent by other Buddhist countries. In a remarkably short period of time, Bhikkhu Kashyap was able to build the Institute both physically and academically and it soon began attracting students from various countries.

Ven. Jagdish Kashyap had been for long thinking of a standard edition of the Tipitaka in Devanagari which could be used by all students of Pali in India. Since things were now moving favourably he started corresponding with both the State and the Central Governments as well as with individuals and institutions. And the right moment came when the Government of India decided to celebrate the Buddha Jayanti to mark the 2500th anniversary of Buddha's Mahaparinirvana. His scheme of publication of the whole Tipitaka in Devanagari was accepted by the Government as a five year project. It was jointly sponsored by the Government of Bihar and the Government of India. It was indeed an ambitious undertaking of organization and scholarship to complete the work of editing and publishing the 41 Volumes in a period of five years. But Bhikkhu Kashyap was a man of great will. The marathon labour which he and his team put in the work is difficult to imagine by those who did not witness it. There were three centres where three teams of his students worked and they all lived in or near the printing presses where the texts were being printed. Ven. Kashyap worked on an average of sixteen to eighteen hours a day. There were incidents and moments during the preparation of the Series that speak of his boldness and pragmatism, generosity, sacrifice, perseverence as well as adventure. He would not brook any obstruction to, and any delay, in the work. Once, when there was some delay in the release of salary and other payments to his workers he sold his house and raised money to disburse the salary of his staff and to make other payments. He did not wait. He was lucky in having a very devoted team of students, who co-operated with him fully. Thus, it was possible to complete this project of great magnitude in the stipulated period of time. The first volume of the series had been brought out in 1956 on the occasion of the Buddha Jayanti and the complete set was ready in 1961. The completion of the project was celebrated at a function held at Sarnath in December 1961 when the first complete set was presented to Jawanar Lal Nehru, the Prime Minister of India.

During the publication of the Devanagari edition of the Pali Tipitaka, Ven. Kashyap had moved to Varanasi, and made it the headquarters of his activities. While the printing was going on, his presence in the city also led the Sanskrit University of Varanasi to ask him to join as the first Professor and Head of the Department of Pali and Buddhism in 1959 and he thus started yet another centre of Pali studies. He remained in Varanasi until 1965 before he returned to Nalanda to rejoin the Directorship of the Nava Nalanda Mahavihara.

While engaged with the publication project of the Tipitaka Ven. Kashyap had also initiated a project on Tipitaka Mahakosha to be done by his team at the Sanskrit University. And when he returned to Nalanda again he started yet another project on Pali Atthakatha under his editorship. His failing health, however, did not permit him, much against his will, to put in the same amount of energy as he had put in the Tipitaka project. He retired from the second term of his Directorship of Nava Nalanda Mahavihara in 1973.

Ven. Jagdish Kashyap considered Buddhism as one movement and he was liberal in outlook. He had already contributed to, and participated in, the activities of the Maha Bodhi Society initially run mainly by the men and money of Sri Lanka. He actively supported the Thai Buddhists at Bodh Gaya, and donated a plot of 1.25 acres of land and six buildings at Nalanda to the Thai Buddhist Sangha in March 1974. Similarly he took active interest in the Japanese Buddhist work in India, Particularly at Rajgir. He had been invited to Japan in 1954 on the occasion of the inauguration of the first Vishva Santi Stupa in Japan. Since then he became friendly with the Venerable Nichidatsu Fujii and took interest in the Nichiren sect and the work of Japan Buddha Sangha in India. In 1970, he became the Vice President of the Bharat-Japan Buddha Sangha. He was very much moved by what happened in Tibet leading to His Holiness the Dalai Lama's refuge in India. He did his best to help, financially and otherwise, the Tibetan refugee monks. He donated lands at Sarnath and at Nalanda for their use. He also helped in the establishment of the Tibetan Institute at the Sanskrit University of Varanasi.

Amidst all his preoccupations, Ven. Kashyap was not oblivious to his responsibilities to the Buddhists and the Buddhist Movement of India. He had been in touch with Dr. B.R. Ambedkar and his movement in Maharashtra from the early fifties, and with similar other movements in Rajasthan and Uttar Pradesh, for the conversion of the people of the lower castes to Buddhism. He even presided over some of the group conversion ceremonies. But he was not a full time participant in these movements ; he could not afford to do so in view of his many commitments which did not permit him sufficient time and the required mobility in those parts of India.

From the beginning, Ven. Kashyap was greatly interested in the meditational practices of Buddhism. Not only did he countinue practising dhyana himself but promoted several schemes for the development and application of Buddhist system of meditation. He had sponsored a scheme to develop a meditational school at Nalanda and also built a dormitory with meditational cells which he later donated to the Thai Buddhists. He also supported the organization of the Vipassana meditational traaining camps in India dirccted by S.N. Goenka.

Ven. Jagdish Kashyap's health for most of his life was robust for he was a man of active habits and he could control his diet, and did exercise. But during the five years period of the editing and publication of the 41 volumes of Tipitaka he did not take care of his health as he wanted to bring out all the volumes within the stipulated time. It was then that he developed diabetes. After he retired from Nalanda in 1973 his general health began deteriorating. In 1974 he became seriously ill at Nalanda. For the next two years, he was more or less immoblised. When in 1975 he finally became bedridden, he decided to live in the Japanese Buddhist Temple at Rajgir. From the window of his room in the Japanese temple he could see the hills of Rajagriha famous in the Budd hist tradition as well as the recently built Peace Pagoda on the Ratnagiri hill. Ven. Jagdish Kashyap passed away on 28 January, 1976, and was cremated with full honours at Nalanda in the vicinity of the Nava Nalanda Mahavihara, the Pali Research Institute created by him.

17

VEN. NANDABANSHA

Venerable Nandabansha Maha Thera, founder of the All Assam Buddhist Association, was born in a Hindu family at Betbari village in the Sibsagar Sub-Division on 15 June 1909. His father died when he was nine years old, and few years later his mother also passed away. Being depressed at the sudden death of his parents, his mind turned towards religion. In search of solace, he began to go through the scriptures of Hinduism. But he found there no real path of salvation. Then per chance he listened to the advices of the Dhammapada from a Sramanera. Thereupon, he became interested in the Buddha-Dhamma. He gave up Hinduism, and embraced Buddhism in 1930 at Rahanpather Buddhist Temple under the influence of Ven. Uttamananda Maha Thera. He studied at Nalanda Vidya Bhavan, Calcutta for three years from 1934-37. In November 1937, he received his higher ordination (Upasampada) at Rahanpather Buddha Vihara under the associated guidance of Ven. Usumangala Maha Thera, Ven. Uttamananda Matha Thera and Ven. Tejabanta Bhikkhu.

In 1939, Ven. Nandabansha came to Desangpani in Sibsagar district, and established a Buddha Vihara there. Same year, he founded the All Assam Buddhist Association in order to unify all the Buddhists of Assam. In 1944, Ven. Nandabansha established the Dhemaji Desangpani Government Aided High School, and established Chala Jnanodaya Pali Vidyalaya in 1948. He also took a leading part in the establishment of Buddha Viharas and Pali Tools (schools) at Pandu, Tinsukhia, Sibsagar, Jorhat, Digboi, Dibrugarh and Shillong. Ven. Nandabansha was also associated with many other religious and social welfare societies.

Ven. Nandabansha was a protific writer and a scholar of reupute. He wrote more than 25 books on Buddhism and history in the Assamese language which made Buddhism more popular in Assam.

18

VEN. DHARMARAKSHITA

Venerable Dharmarakshita was born in a small hamlet near Kushinagar, the site of Lord Buddha's Maha-parinirvana, on Ist April 1923. He was in the first batch of students who joined the Primary school established at Kushinagar in 1929 by Venerable U Chandramani Maha Thera. He passed the High School Examination in First Division with distinction in Pali. After graduating from the Buddha College, Kushinagar, he joined the Banaras Hindu University,, Varanasi, from where he obtained the degree of Master of Arts. He was awarded the Ph.D. degree by the Ranchi University for his Thesis on "Buddha Yoga Sadhana".

While still in the high school, he showed his inclination toward Buddhism, and spent most of his time at Kushinagar in the company of Ven. Chandramani. At the age of 19, he renounced home and became a Samanera, with the premission of his parents, on 28 July 1942. He received his higher ordination, Upasampada, on 21 July 1944 from Ven. Chandramani Maha Thera and eleven other Buddhist monks from Burma, in the Seema built at Kushinagar. Soon after this, Ven. Dharmarakshita left for Sri Lanka to study the Tripitaka and the Pali literature at the Maha Matinda Oriental College. At this great seat of Buddhist learning, he studied under the able guidance of Ven'ble Dhammavasa Sanghanayaka Maha Thera, and was awarded the degree of Tripitakacharya in recognition of his distinguished scholarship.

On return from Sri Lanka, he continued to pursue his studies in Hindi and Urdu. He passed the Visharad and Sahitya-Ratana Examinations of the Banaras Hindu University and also passed the Urdu-Ala and Munshi examination of Anjaman Islamia Madarasa, a seat of Urdu learning at Gorakhpur. He also made a deep study of the Vedas and Puranas at the Bhartiya Veda Vidyalaya, Kanpur, and was awarded the degree of Dharmashastri by that institution.

Having equipped himself with so many degrees and having gained deep knowledge of Buddhism, Ven. Dharmarakshita joined the Maha Bodhi Society of India as a Dhammaduta worker. He spent most of his life at Sarnath, the Holy Isipatana, and served the Dhamma in various ways. For a number of years, he was Editor of Dharmaduta, the Hindi monthly organ of the Maha Bodhi Society published from Sarnath. During his editorship, 'Dharmaduta' became a premier Buddhist journal in Hindi and helped a great deal in popularising the Buddha-Dhamma amongst the Hindi knowing masses.

Bhikshu Dharmarakshita was an eminent educationist. For about a decade he was Lecturer of Pali at the Maha Bodhi College, Sarnath. In December 1959, he became Principal of that College, and held that post, with distinction, for more than 15 years. He was also a member of the Varanaseya Sanskrit University, Varanasi, and a Research Guide of the Agra University. He was also on the Pali Committee of the Intermediate Board, U.P., besides being the examiner of M.A. and B.A. examinations of some other Universities in India.

Ven. Dharmarakshita was one of the distinguished invitees to the Sixth Great Buddhist Council held in Burma in 1956, and was selected as a 'Dharma Samgayaka'. He also participated in the World Fellowship of Buddhists Conference held in Burma in 1954. He was also actively associated with the Kushinagar Bhikshu Sangha, Vaishali Sangha, and Bhartiya Bhikshu Sangha.

Ven. Dharmarakshita had known Dr. B. R. Ambedkar since 1943. He writes : "It happened in 1943. I was in my room in the Kushinagar Vihara, and was absorbed in editing my book' 'Jati-bhed aur Buddha'. The time was nine O'clock in the morning. Two persons entered the room from the western door and just stood by the side of my table. Raising my head a little, I saw Acharya Medharthi of Kanpur with another tall person, of fair complex and towering personality. I asked, 'When did you come ?'.

'We are just coming. He is Dr. Bhim Rao Ambedkar', replied Acharya Medharthi.

On hearing this, I was wonder-struck. Dr. Ambedkar, the emancipator of the downtrodden, whose speeches and writings I was so fond of reading, was standing before me in person.

'What are you writing ?', asked Dr. Ambedkar.

'Whatever references about caste-system are there in the Tripitaka, I am collecting them and translating the same into Hindi', I replied.

'Very Good', I want such Bhikkhus. Keep on writing and preaching the Dhamma. As soon as the manuscript is ready, send it to Sant Ram in Lahore mentioning my name, it will be published by the Jat-Pat Todak Mandal', said Dr. Ambedkar in an assuring tone". Ven. Dharmarakshita records that after completing the book, he sent the manuscript to Lahore, as directed by Dr. Ambedkar, and it was published without any delay.

When Dr. Ambedkar finally launched mass Buddhist revival movement in October 1956, Ven. Dharmarakshita extended his whole-hearted co-operation. Last time, he met Dr. Ambedkar was during the latter's visit to Sarnath in November 1956. In fact, all arrangements for Babasaheb's three days stay at Sarnath from 22—24 November were made by him. An interesting description of his three meetings with Dr. Ambedkar in 1943 (at Kushinagar), 1954 (in Burma) and 1956 (at Sarnath) has been given by Ven. Dharmarakshita in the book 'Baudh Dharm he Manav Dharm', a collection of speeches of Dr. Ambedkar, compiled by him. He endeavoured to give maximum push to the revival movement. He even wrote some books in Marathi for the benefit of the people of Maharashtra.

Bhikshu Dharmarakshita was a reputed Buddhist scholar, and had written more than 50 treatises on Buddhism in Hindi and Pali. The books and pamphlets written by him are : Samyutta Nikaya-Two parts (Hindi translation), Dhammapada (Hindi only), Dhammapada (Pali-Hindi) and Dhammapada (Text, Translation with legends), Iti Vutaka (Pali-Hindi). Mahaparinirvana Sutta (Pali-Hindi), Sutta-Nipata (Pali-Hindi) Visuddhimagga (Hindi translation in two parts), Jataka Atthakatha—Part I (Pali), Carriya-Pitaka (Pali-Hindi), Nidana-Katha (Pali-Hindi), Tela-Katha Gatha (Pali-Hindi), Loka-Niti (Pali-Hindi), Pali Patha Mala (Pali), Pali Veyakarana, Pali Sahitya ka Ithas, Bhikshu Patimoksha, Sramner Vinaya, Baudh Dharm ke Updesh, Tathagata Hridya, Jati-bhed aur Buddha, Baudh Yogi ke Patra, Tathagata ke Pratham Updesh, Acharya Buddha-Ghosh, Baudh Shishu Bodh, Baudh Charyavidhi, Baudh Dharm ke Mul-sidhant, Om Mani Padme Hum, Mahavanso (translation) Baudh Kahaniyan, Baudh Dharm Darshan Tatha Ithas, Dhammapada Attha-Katha, Buddha-Vansha, Panch-sheel Katha, Baudh Sadhna, Baudh Sanskar Padhiti, Buddha ka Pratham Sandesh, Katha Vatthuppakaran, Baudh Vibhutian, Lanka Yatra, Nepal Yatra, Kushinagar ka Ithas, Sarnath-Varansi, Kushinagar Dig Darshan, Sarnath ka Ithas, Sarnath Dig Darshan, Baudh-Kalin Bharat ka Bhaugolik Parichaya, Kalama Gantantra ka Kesaputra, Miliuda Prashana Marathi), Pali Sahitya ki Rup Rekha (Urdu).

For his service to Pali and Buddhism, Venerable Dharmarakshita was honoured by the Nava Nalanda Mahavihara in 1971 by conferring upon him an honorary degree of Vidyavaridhi (D. Litt.). Such a great scholar, educationist and missionary monk passed away at the age of 54 on 23 May 1977.

19

VEN. L. ARIYAWANSA

Ven. Lakhera Ariyawansa Nayaka Maha Thera was born on 23 October 1915, the Ashvina full-moon day, in a respectable Barua Buddhist family of the village Lakhera in Chittagong District of Bengal (now in Bangladesh). Apurva, as he he was named by his parents, received his early education in his native place. He was ordained as a Samanera in 1982 by Ven. Pragyalankar Maha Thera, the Sanghanayaka of Chittagong. Soon thereafter, he joined the Maha Muni Pali Bodhi Niketan and began learning Pali from Ven. Dharmaloka Maha Thera. In 1930, Ariyawansa along with his Guru, Ven. Pragyalankar, and his father, came on pilgrimage to the sacred Buddhist shrines in North India. During this pilgrimage, he per chance, met at Sarnath the Ven. Moligoda Ariyawansa Maha Nayaka Thera of Sri Lanka who had also come to India on pilgrimage. At their very first meeting, Ariyawansa of India expressed his wish to study under the Ven. Ariyawansa of Sri Lanka. His request was promptly accepted by the Maha Nayaka Thera who promised to make arrangements for young Ariyawansa's visit to Sri Lanka as soon as possible.

After the pilgrimage, Ariyawansa returned to his home in Chittagong and continued his studies in Pali and Buddhism. In 1931, he was invited by Devapriya Valisinha, whom he had met during the course of his pilgrimage, to join the newly established Bhikkhu Training School at Sarnath where a batch of ten Samaneras brought from Sri Lanka by Anagarika Dharmapala were getting training. Ariyawansa joined the Sarnath Institute on 16 June 1931 and began learning Pali and Sinhalese from Ven D. Sasanasiri Maha Thera. Just after a year, in July 1932, Ariyawansa, having received an invitation from Sri Lanka took leave from Sarnath ; went back to Chittagong and from there sailed to the Island via Rangoon.

After joining the Pravachanodaya Oriental College at Molligoda, L. Ariyawansa made a deep study of Pali Tripitaka and Sinhali language and literature for nine years under the able guidance of

Ven. Molligoda Ariyawansa Maha Nayaka Thera, Principal of the College and the Chief incumbent of the Kotte Raja-Mahavihara. Ven. L. Ariyawansa received his higher ordination (Upasampada) in June 1938 from the Sangha led by Ven. M. Ariyawansa Maha Nayaka Thera. He completed his studies in 1941 and obtained the highest degree of Sri Saddharmacharya.

In December 1941, after meritorious stay of nine and a half years at the Pravachanodaya Pirivena in Sri Lanka, Ven. L. Ariyawansa returned to his motherland and began to work as a Dhamma preacher. Keen to understand the Buddha Dhamma in all its glory, he continued his studies on return to India also. During the period from 1942 to 1945 he passed all the examinations of Sutta, Vinaya and Abhidhamma and attained the degree of Tripitaka Visharda of the Bengal Sanskrit Association. Next four years he spent at the Abhaya Vihara at his native place in Chittagong serving the Dhamma and social needs of the people.

On an invitation from Devapriya Valisinha, General Secretary of the Maha Bodhi Society of India, Ven. Ariyawansa joined the Maha Bodhi Society as a Dhammaduta worker in October 1949. He assisted the Society for some time at Calcutta and Sarnath. In November 1950, he took over from Ven. Dr. H. Saddhatissa Maha Thera, as Bhikkhu in-charge of the New Delhi Buddha Vihara.

Ever since his arrival in the capital of India, Ven. Ariyawansa has been actively engaged in a wide range of Buddhist activities, such as, celebration of Buddha Jayanti and other sacred days in proper style and form, organisation of seminars, lectures and sermons on Buddhism, reception to prominent visiting Buddhists from India and abroad, and publication of Buddhist literature. His contacts with National leaders like Dr. B.R. Ambedkar, Jawaharlal Nehru, Dr. Rajendra Prasad, Dr. Kailash Nath Katju and others helped the cause of Buddhism to a great extent. He was instrumental in having the Buddha Purnima, Thrice Sacred Day, declared as a Public holiday in 1953 by the Government of India. He was also closely associated with the 2500th Buddha Jayanti functions organised by the Government. It was also primarily at his instance that in 1964 Mrs. Sirimavo Bandaranaike, Prime Minister of Sri Lanka brought a Bo sapling from the historic Bodhi Tree at Anuradhapura for being planted in the Buddha Jayanti Park in New Delhi to commemmorate the Birth Cenetenary of Anagarika Dharmpala, the founder of the Maha Bodhi Society. This sacred Bo-sapling was planted on 25 October 1964 by Lal Bahadur Shastri, the then Prime Minister of India, and is now a flourishing Bo-tree venerated by the Buddhists. Ven. Ariyawansa was also responsible for establishing Jagajjoyti Vihara in South Delhi in 1968 for the benefit of the Bangali Buddhist community.

Ven. Ariyawansa has written a number of books, pamphlets and articles in English, Hindi and Bengali. His first book Subodhalankar was originally written in Pali while he was still in Sri Lanka. It was translated into Bengali and published from Calcutta in 1948. It is even now prescribed in the syllabus of M.A. of the Calcutta University. It is also prescribed in the syllabus of Shastri of Assam Sanskrit Board. Among the other popular books and pamphlets written by him for wider circulation, mention may be made of : Buddha Niti Shikska Karya (Bengali), Buddhanushan (Hindi), Baudha Upasana Tatha Mangala Paddhiti (Hindi) and Baudha Jeevan Path (Hindi-co-author, D.C. Ahir).

For his valuable services to the Dhamma, Ven. L. Ariyawansa was honoured in 1979 with the title of Chief Sangha Nayaka of North India by the Kotte Mangala Uposathagara Kalyani Samagri Dharma Maha Sangha Sabha, Sri Lanka.

Presently, Ven. Ariyawansa is the Vice-President of the Maha Bodhi Society of India. He is also associated with a number of other organisations is India and abroad ; prominent among them being the World Buddhist Sangha, and Asian Buddhist Conference for Promoting Peace. He has also been appointed as the International Honorary Adviser to the International Buddhist Research Institute, Seol, Korea. He has travelled widely in India and abroad. In 1978, he attended the World Fellowship of Buddhists as a Chief Guest in Japan at the invitation of the Japan Buddhist Association. In October 1985, he led an Indian Buddhist delegation to China.

By now, Ven. L. Ariyawansa has completed 38 years of meritorious Dhamma service in the Capital of India. His sweetness of behaviour, hospitable nature, clear understanding of others' needs, intelligent transmission of the teachings of the Buddha, through speech and writing, and from the conferences in the international sphere, have won him innumberable disciples, all devotedly attached to him and through him to the Dhamma. He has been thus a Dhammaduta par excellence.

20

VEN. KUSHAK BAKULA

Ven. Kushak Bakula, the Head Lama of Ladakh, was born on 19 May 1917, the Vaisakha Purnima day, in the royal family of Matho, Ladakh in Jammu and Kashmir State On being recognised as the re-incarnation of the previous Head Lama, and 20th re-incarnation of Arhat 'Bakul', he was brought with full honours to the Spituk Gompa (monastery), near Leh. After initial education, he went at the age of 12 to pursue higher religious education and training at the Depung Monastery in Lhasa, Tibet. He studied there for 14 years and received 'Geshe Lharampa', the highest degree in Buddhist studies and Metaphysics, securing the first position in the Institution. He is specialised in the Mahayana school of thought.

Ven. Kushak Bakula is a great missionary and has revitalised Buddhism in Ladakh to a great extent. He has not only engaged himself in ecelesiastical activities with utmost devotion and dedication but has also taken keen interest in tackling the socio-economic problems of the Ladakhis. Besides being the head of the Pethub Monastery, he is also associated with a number of other religious and educational institutions. Consequent on Chinese occupation of Tibet, he has made arrangements for imparting traditional and modern education to Buddhist monks in India itself to keep alive the rich cultural heritage of Buddhism in Ladakh. The impressive Ladakh Buddha Vihara, Delhi, established in 1963, is also the result of Ven. Kushak Bakula's initiative and interest in the welfare of his people.

Ven. Kushak Bakula is a scholar of repute of the Tibetan language, and has written a number of commentaries on Buddhist philosophy and metaphysics. Widely travelled, he has participated in many Conferences of the World Fellowship of Buddhists as well as International Conference on peace, disarmament and aparthied. He is the Vice-President of the Asian Buddhist Council for Peace, and is also on the Board of Management and Presidium of many other national and international bodies.

Considering the strategic importance of Ladakh region and its need for a leader, he, at the instance of Jawaharlal Nehru, plunged into active politices in 1949, and while leading an ascetic life, has dominated Ladakh's political scene for over three decades at State and Central levels. He was a member of the Jammu and Kashmir State Legislative Assembly from 1951-1967 and a Minister in the J & K. Government for 14 years during which period he held the portfolios of : Deputy Minister for Ladakh Affairs (1953-57) ; Minister of State for Ladakh Affairs and Trade Agencies (1957-62) ; and Minister of State for Health, Local Self-Government, Ladakh Affairs and Trade Agencies (1964-1967). After his long innings in the State affairs, he was elected from Ladakh to the Fourth Lok Sabha (1967-70), and was elected again to the Fifth Lok Sabha (1971-77). Presently, he is a Member of the Minorities' Commission of India.

In his dual capacity as a respected religious leader and as a political activist, Ven. Kushak Bakula has made significant contribution in consolidating the secular forces in the sensitive Ladakh region, and bringing its people within the national mainstream. Recognising his 'very useful' role in public affairs, he was honoured by the Government of India by Padma Bhushan on the occasion of Republic Day in 1988.

21

AYODHYA DASA

With the establishment of the head office of the Theosphical Society in India at Adyar, Madras, Colonel H. S. Olcott became a frequent visitor to Madras. Since he had embraced Buddhism in Ceylon, which had attracted world-wide attention, the Untouchables, the Panchamas as they were called in South India, were also attracted towards Buddhism. When in June 1898, Col. Olcott and Anagarika Dharmapala visited Adyar, a delegation of the Panchamas met them and sought admission to Buddhism. Dharmapala in his diary jottings for 4 June 1898 records : "The Panchamas, descendents of ancient Buddhists, called on Colonel to present there petition to admit them as Buddhists". Dharmapala further records on 7 June, "In the evening the Panchama meeting held in Raypettah. Col. Olcott and the old priest and myself represented the Buddhists. An intelligent body of men they were. Buddha's Dhamma is above caste and the Panchamas will be raised from their degraded condition and the influence of the Dhamma shown".

These Panchamas or the Untouchables were led by an enlightened person, Pandit Ayodhya Dasa or Ayoti Dasa. He was the first person to embrace Buddhism in 1898 itself. In order to give practical shape to his ideas—to gain freedom from slavery and serfdom, to cast away Hinduism in which there was nothing for the Panchamas except hatred, abhorence and humiliation, Pandit Ayodhya Dasa founded in 1900 the South India Buddhist Association at Perambur, Madras. This Association is still holding aloft the banner of Dhamma in the South. Pandit Ayodhya Dass wrote an important work in Tamil titled 'Buddharadam Adivedam'. He also edited for a number of years the Weekly Tamil Bulletin 'Tamlian' on behalf of the South India Buddhist Association, which ceased, publication few years after his demise in 1914.

22

P. LAKSHMI NARASU

Professor P. Lakshmi Narasu was a graduate in Physics from the Madras Christian College. In 1897 he was appointed as Assistant Professor of Physics and Chemistry at the same College. Being an able, honest and hard working teacher, he was very popular with his students. His eminence as an educationist was recognised soon, and before long he was appointed as Principal of the Pachiappa's College.

Prof. Narasu was a great admirer of Buddhism and gave lectures on the subject almost every weakend. He was known to Anagarika Dharampala, and in the year 1900, he, together with M. Singaravelu, opened a branch of the Maha Bodhi Society in Madras He also managed for some time, on behalf of the Maha Bodhi Society, a school hall at Perambur, Madras for the clementary education of "Dravidian Buddhist children". Being more interested in the revival of Buddhism in practical terms, he later actively collaborated with the South India Buddhist Association, of which he became President, after the demise of Pandit Ayodhya Dasa, its founder.

Prof. Narasu was a prolific writer and logician. His book 'The Essence of Buddhism' which was first published in 1907, again in 1911, and then again in 1948 and 1976 is by any standard the best book on Buddhism and comparative study of other religions. His command over the subject and the language is marvellous. At one place, he says : Dogma and miracle are wisdom to the Christians; kismet and fanaticism are wisdom to the Moslem; caste and ceremonialism are wisdom to the Brahmin; asceticism and nakedness are wisdom to the Jain; mysticism and magic are wisdom to the Taoist; formalism and outward piety are wisdom to the Confucian; ancestor-worship and loyality to the Mikado are wisdom to the Shinitoist; but love and piety are the first wisdom to the Buddhist".

Dr. B. R. Ambedkar liked Prof. Narasu's book so much that he recommended it for study to his followers, and himself wrote a Preface, giving a brief life-sketch of the author, while getting its third edition published in 1948. Dr. Ambedkar hailed Prof. Narasu as "a prodigy of the last century", and paid tribute to him in the following words :

"Prof. Narasu was a social Reformer. He fought caste to the best of his ability and raised the standard of Revolt against its tyranny in Hinduism, so early as in the nineties of the 19th century. He was a great admirer of Buddhism and gave courses of lectures on the subject week in and week out. He was highly popular with his students over whom he exercised a magical personal influence so as to broaden their outlook and widen their visions. His sense of self-respect both personal and national was of a high order and he did not stand the arrogance and sense of self-superiority of his European colleagues to whom he was always ready to give their due in the domain of scholarship but at whose hands he would not take insults lying down".

"Prof. Narasu was a highly public-spirited citizen and took active part in the organisation of a body known as the 'National Fund and Industrial Association' under whose auspices, petty donations were being collected with which aid was rendered to students who desired to go abroad for advanced technical education. Japan was the country which attracted the young men of the day and it was their ambition to learn the technique of various small industries and manufactures-notably-soap making, enamelling and paints manufacture and so on. But the Professor's one sin was social reform and in Buddhism he found his solace. He was one of the earliest to discern the evils of the caste system, early marriages and prohibition of widow marriage and it was then considered in Reform Circles a matter for gratification that one of his brothers was practical Social Reformer, having married a widow. That was the era when Christian Missionaries were not only countenancing the social reform movement but viewed it with high favour as making a half-way house between orthodox Hinduism and conversion to Christianity. It did not take long for them to change their views and look upon such progressive movements as constituting a real hindrance to proselytization.'!

"Prof. Narasu was the stalwart of the 19th century who had fought European arrogance with patriotic fervour, orthodox Hinduism with inconoclastic zeal, heterodox Brahmins with nationalistic vision and aggressive Christianity with a rationalistic outlook—all under the inspiring banner of his unflagging faith in the teachings of the Great Buddha".

Prof. Narasu wrote another popular book 'What is Buddhism' which serves as a brief but 'very useful' introduction to Buddhism. This small book is also still widely read.

Professor Lakshmi Narasu passed away in 1934.

23

C. KRISHNAN

C. Krishnan, Editor of the 'Mitavadi' published from Calicut, was the first pioneer Buddhist in Kerala. He was from the Izhava caste and had embraced Buddhism in the early 1920's. On 9 February 1920, he organised the first All Kerala Buddhist Conference which was inaugarated by M. R. Iyer and was presided over by C. Jinarajadasa. A Kerala Buddhist Association was formed at this Conference, with C. Krishnan as President. Two years later, on 16 May 1927, a Buddhist Temple was opened at Calicut in a building at Paran Square donated by Krishnan. Ven. Dharmakhanda, who was the first Malayali to become a Buddhist monk, later joined hands with Krishnan and gave further impetus to the revival of Buddhism in Kerala.

At the request of C. Krishnan, the Maha Bodhi Society of India sent in August 1935 a Buddhist mission to Calicut under the leadership of Ven. Ananda Maitreya. The mission carried on a strenuous campaign, visited many towns, and addressed many meetings in the State. Same year, C. Krishnan, who was now Member Legislative Council, was elected as President of the Malabar Branch of the Maha Bodhi Society. Through his generousity, the Maha Bodhi Society established in 1937 in Calicut the 'Maha Bodhi Vihara' to meet the needs of the growing number of Buddhists. Having served the Dhamma with devotion and dedication for about two decades, C. Krishnan passed away in 1939.

24

DR. ANANDRAO NAIR

Dr. Anandrao L. Nair, a well-known medical practioner and philanthropist of Bombay, pioneered the Buddhist revival movement in the capital of Maharashtra. Inspired by the sublime teachings of the Buddha, he founded the Buddha Society on 1st May 1922, with himself as President and S. H. Jhabvala as Secretary. Under the aupices of this Society, he organised the Buddha Jayanti celebrations every year in Bombay and also arranged lectures by eminent Buddhist scholars from time to time. In 1931, Dr. Nair built the first Buddha Vihara in the compound of his hospital in Bombay, and bore its entire cost. With the establishment of Ananda Vihara, as it is now known, the Buddhist revival movement received further impetus in Western India. Expanding its activities, the Society organised the Dhammapada classes for the benefit of the younger generation. These private classes were taken by Prof. N K. Bhagwat, who co-operted fully with Dr. Nair in his efforts to popularise Buddhism in this part of the country. In 1933, Dr. Nair founded the journal 'Buddha Prabha' with a view to spreading the Dhamma far and wide. His dreams were, however, cut short by his untimely death in 1934.

After Dr. Nair's death, the journal 'Buddha Prabha' was published for a few years by K. A. Padhye. Later, the Ananda Vihara was handed over to the Maha Bodhi Society of India, and is still serving the Dhamma.

25

SHEO NARAIN

Rai Bahadur Pandit Sheo Narain Shamim was a leading advocate of the Punjab High Court, Lahore, in the 1920's. He was a devout Buddhist and a great friend of Anagarika Dharmapala, the founder of the Maha Bodhi Society of India. His residence in Lahore was known as 'Kapilavastu.' Such was the impact of the Buddha's teachings on him that he could not be swayed by the forceful Arya Samaj movement then emerging in Punjab. Rahul Sankrityayan, who had known him personally, records[1] that Pandit Sheo Narain Shamim writing about Swami Dayanand, founder of the Arya Samaj, once said : I had seen Swamiji, I had heard his lectures; but my head and heart had already been captivated by the Buddha, hence I could not become an Arya Samaji".

Pandit Sheo Narain did his utmost to popularise Buddhism through literature. He contributed a number of articles to the 'Maha Bodhi' journal. His three pamphlets in English, namely, Asoka, Sarnath a Guide, and Buddhism, published by the Maha Bodhi Society of India were popular for a long time. He also published a booklet on Buddhism in Urdu for the benefit of the masses. He was also representative of the Maha Bodhi Society at Lahore for more than a decade. When in 1931, the Mulagandhakuti Vihara, built by Anagarika Dharmapala, was consecrated and the Vihara Library was being organised, he gladly gifted his collection of books on Buddhism to the new library. Such a pioneer Punjabi Buddhist passed away at Lahore in 1936.

---

1. Navadeekshit Baudh, Lucknow, 1957, p. 3.

26

N. K. BHAGWAT

Born in 1887, Professor N.K. Bhagwat had a distinguished academic carrer. A disciple of the great Dharmananda Kosambi, he took keen interest in the Buddhist revival movement in Bombay, and was one of the small band of devoted scholars who, from the beginning of the 20th century, kept the torch of Pali and Buddhistic studies burning in Western India. He was Professor of Pali at St. Xavier College in Bombay. Besides occupying with distinction various academic posts, Prof. Bhagwat edited a number of Pali texts in Devanagari characters, and translated Dhammapada and some other Pali works. An important original work written by him was 'The Buddhist Philosophy of Theravada School'. He was also a frequent contributor to religious and culture journals. For many years he himself edited and published the journal 'Dharma Chakra': 'the Wheel of the Moral Law'.

A popular speaker, Prof. Bhagwat was closely associated in his younger days with Dr. Anandrao Nair, the founder of the Ananda Vihara, Bombay. He often lectured at the Ananda Vihara and also taught Dhammapada in private classes by the Buddha Society for the benefit of the younger generation. He was also an ardent champion of social reforms, and upto the very last he maintained an active interest in the various social welfare societies.

Prof. N.K Bhagwat passed away at the age of 75 on 20 April 1962. At the time of death he was Head of the Department of Pali in the Siddharth College, Bombay, a premier institution established by Dr. B.R. Ambedkar.

27

DR. B. M. BARUA

Dr. Beni Madhab Barua, a great Indologist and an acknowledged authority on Buddhism, was born on 31 December 1888 in a Barua Buddhist family of the village of Mahamuni Pahartali in the Chittagong district of undivided Bengal (now in Bangladesh). In 1911, he graduated in first division from the Calcutta University with honours in Pali. In 1913, he passed the M.A. examination standing first class in Pali. Then in 1914, with the help of Ven. Kripasaran Mahathera, founder of the Bengal Buddhist Association, and Sir Ashutosh Mookerjee, Vice-Chancellor of the Calcutta University, he proceeded to England as a State Scholar for further studies and joined the University of London. In 1917, he was awarded the degree of Doctor of Literature (D. Litt.) by the University of London for his thesis entitled 'Indian Philosophy—Its original growth from the Vedas to the Buddha.' On return to India Dr. Barua was appointed in December 1917 as Lecturer of Pali in the University of Calcutta. He was elevated to the post of Professor of Pali in 1925 and served in that capacity with distinction till his death in 1948. Dr. Barua was also attached with the departments of Sanskrit and Ancient Indian History and Culture of the Calcutta University. He was also an external examiner of a number of Universities in India, Burma and Sri Lanka.

Dr. Barua was one of the greatest pioneer Buddhist scholars. He published a number of learned and monumental works on different aspects of Buddhism ; notable among them being : A History of Pre-Buddhistic Indian Philosophy ; A Prolegomena to a History of Buddhist Philosophy : The Ajivakas ; Bharhut Inscriptions ; Prakrit Dhammapada ; Gaya and Budhagaya ; Bharhut (in 3 volumes) ; Inscriptions of Asoka (2 volumes) ; Asoka and His Inscriptions. His last book 'Philosophy of Progress' was published after his death. Dr. Barua also contributed more than 75 well researched papers to various journals and conferences in the country. He also published some books on Buddhism in Bengali.

Dr. Barua worked in close co-operation with the Bengal Buddhist Association for the revival of Buddhism in India. He served for sometime as Secretary of the Association. He was Chairman of the Reception Committee of All India Buddhist Conference held at Calcutta in 1928. He was also President of the Nalanda Vidya-Bhavan established by the Bengal Buddhist Association in 1935 for the teaching of Pali and Buddhism. He also edited Jagajjyoti, a journal published by the Association since 1908. He was also Editor of Buddhist India and one of the founder Editors of Indian Culture.

Dr. Barua visited Sri Lanka in 1944 and delivered a series of lectures on Buddhism in various institutions. The Vidyalankara Pirivena (now University) of Sri Lanka conferred upon him the title of Tipitakacariya in recognition of the conspicious services rendered by him to the cause of Buddhism and Buddhistic studies. He also visited Burma four times, in 1924, 1927, 1937 and 1938, and delivered a number of lectures at various places.

Dr. Barua was associated with many public institutions and societies. He was the co-founder of the Indian Research Institute and founder of the Jogendra—Rupasibala Tripitaka Trust Board He also served as a member of the managing committees of a number of institutions, such as, the Maha Bodhi Society of India, Bangiya Sahitya Parishad, the Bharati Mahavidyalaya of Calcutta and Vidyalankara Pirivena of Sri Lanka. Dr. Barua was elected a Fellow of the Royal Asiatic Society of Bengal and was awarded Dr. B.C. Law Gold Medal by the Society. He was elected President of the Prakrit section of the All India Oriental Conference at its Tirupati session in 1944 ; President of the Indian section of the Indian History Congress at its Annamalainagar session in 1945 ; and also a sectional President of the Indian Philosophical Congress held in Delhi in 1946.

Such a talented pioneer Buddhist scholar, Dr. B.M. Barua, passed away on 23 March 1948.

28

THE CHOGYAL OF SIKKIM

The Chogyal of Sikkim, Dr. Palden Thondup Namgyal, was born at Gangtok on 22 May 1923. He was the second son of His Highness the Maharaja Tashi Namgyal of Sikkim. He had his education in Darjeeling, Kalimpong and Simla. After the untimely death of his elder brother, he began assisting his father in State affairs. In 1944, he was selected as the President of the Sikkim State Council, an office he held until 1949. In his capacity as Maharaj Kumar, the Heir Apparent, he exercised direct personal supervision over various departments of the Government of Sikkim. On the death of his father, on 3 December 1963, he ascended the throne of Sikkim. His coronation took place at Gangtok on 4 April 1965 at a colourful ceremony performed in the Royal Chapel in keeping with the age-old tradition.

The Chogyal, then Maharaj Kumar of Sikkim, was elected President of the Maha Bodhi Society of India on 7 October 1953, and he held this high office life-long through re-elections. As a devout Buddhist, he did his level best to help and guide the Maha Bodhi Society in its multifarious activities. In 1956, he was appointed as a member of the Committee constituled by the Government of India to organise the 2500th Buddha Jayanti Celebrations. In 1958, he, under the patronage of his father, founded the Namgyal Institute of Tibetology at Gangtok. He was also associated with a number of religious and educational institutions in India,

During the British rule, Sikkim was a Protectorate of India. This position continued after Independence also till May 1975 when the Protectorate status was withdrawn by the Government of India, and the tiny Buddhist Kingdom merged with India as its twenty-second State. The Chogyal died on 29 January 1982 in New York where he had gone for treatment. His last rites were performed on 19 February 1982 at Gangtok, the capital of Sikkim.

29

DR. R. L. SONI

DR. R.L. Soni was born in June 1904 in a well-to-do Hindu family of Bajwara in district Hoshiarpur, Punjab. Rup Lal spent his early childhood in East Africa (Zanzibar) where his father. Dr. D.D Soni, was a Medical Officer. After graduating in medicine and surgery in 1929 from King Edward Medical College, Lahore (Punjab), Dr. R.L. Soni visited Burma for his honeymoon. The Buddhist atmosphere of that countary made such an immediate and profound impression on his mind that he decided to stay on, soon making a name for himself as a sound Physician.

Dr. Soni was a free thinker. His search for something abiding in religion culminated in his conversion to Buddhism in January 1933 by Venerable Lokanatha, the world renowned Italian Buddhist monk. Impressed by the ethical grandeur, scientific outlook and spiritual vision of Buddhism, Dr. Soni resolved to share his delight with others. The first major step he took in this direction was to organise the Buddhist Foreign Mission which conducted a World Buddhist Survey in 1947-51, under the leadership of Venerable Lokanatha. In 1950, he founded the World Institute of Buddhist Culture at Mandalay, which became a premier institution devoted to the propagation of Buddhism as an instrument of human welfare and world peace. He was also intimately connected with the World Fellowship of Buddhists since its inception, and chaired its Dhammaduta Committee in Sri Lanka (1950) and Cambodia (1961). He also lectured on Buddhism in many parts of Asia. In 1956, he presided over the Maha Buddha Jayanti Celebrations in East Pakistan (now Bangladesh) and was in the panel of Presidents in the World Conference on the Cultivation of the Human Spirit held in Japan in 1961.

A prolific writer and an author of distinction, Dr. Soni wrote a number of books, booklets, pamphlets and leaflets on Buddhist history, philosophy and culture which had a wide circulation. Two of his books merit special notice. His book "Life's Highest Blessings—The High Road to Success and Happiness" which is a translation of, and commentary on the Mahamangla Sutta, details a practical programme of ethico-spiritual culture in the context of modern conditions. The other book "A Cultural Study of the Burmese Era" embodies his researches on the Buddhist Era in the context of the cultural influences in Asia. His third book worthy of note is "The Only Way to Deliverance" published in America in 1980. He was also in the Editorial Board of the Mandalay Monthly 'The Light of Buddha' and was the Buddhist Editor of 'France-Asie', Tokyo.

Though in Burma, Dr. Soni was yearning for the revival of Buddhism in India. When, in 1935, Dr. B.R. Ambedkar announced his intention to leave 'Hinduism', Dr. Soni requested Venerable Lokanatha, his Guru, to meet and try to persuade Dr. Ambedkar to adopt the way of the Buddha to emancipate the downtrodden masses of India. His association with Dr. Ambedkar became more intimate in 1950 when both the leaders participated in the first Conference of the World Fellowship of Buddhists held in Sri Lanka. Significantly enough, the fateful decision of embracing Buddhism in 1956 was taken by Dr. Ambedkar at the residence of Dr. Soni at Mandalay, Burma when he was his guest for about a week in December 1954. When Dr. Ambedkar finally embraced Buddhism on 14 October 1956 and gave a clarion call to his followers to seek refuge in the Buddha Dhamma, Dr. Soni was the happiest man. And after the sudden demise of Dr. Ambedkar in December 1956, he endeavoured to sustain the revival movement by issuing a number of pamphlets and leaflets on Buddhism in English, Hindi, Urdu and Punjabi for free distribution in India. He also activated a good deal of Dhammaduta work through his personal contacts and correspondence. He also addressed a number of Buddhist gatherings in India from time to time During his last tour of India Dr, Soni addressed the National Convention of Buddhists held in New Delhi on 11-12 April 1981, and lectured at Chandigarh, Nalanda and Calcutta. His intense devotion and dedication to

Dhamma made Dr. Soni a radiant of light and inspiration to the Buddhist workers in India.

Dr. R.L. Soni was a born Dhammāduta who spent much of his time, energy and money to promote Buddhism throughout the world. In particular, he was anxious to see Buddhism in India to its full glory. He often said, "no doubt Buddhism needs India but more than that India needs Buddhism". He had plannad to shift to the land of his birth in 1975, the year in which the Maha Bodhi Society published 'Dr. Soni Number' in honour of his Platinum jubilee, and work for the promotion of Dhamma with greater force but this was not to be. Certain practical difficulties forced him to stay on in Burma where he passed away on 27 April 1982, without realising his cherished desire "to die in India serving the Buddha".

Dr. B. R. AMBEDKAR
1891—1956

30

DR. B.R. AMBEDKER

Dr. Bhimrao Ramji Ambedkar was born in a respectable Mahar family of Ambavade, a small village, five miles off Madangad, in Kheda taluka of Ratnagiri district in Maharashtra. His grand father, Maloji Sakpal, was a retired military person from the Bombay Army of the East India Company. His father, Ramji Sakpal, too was in military service and had attained the rank of Subedar Major. Ambedkar's mother, Bhimabai, hailed from the village of Murbad in the Thana district of Maharashtra.

At the time of Ambedkar's birth, his parents were residing at Mhow in Central India, where Ramji Sakpal was serving as Headmaster in the Army school. As in the case of Lord Buddha, a prophecy had also been made prior to the birth of Ambedkar that he would be a great man. It is said that one of the uncles of Ramji Sakpal, who had turned a Sanyasi, once came to Mhow, alongwith some other hermits. Ramji Sakpal happened to meet him and entreated the Sanyasi to bless his house with a visit. The Sanyasi declined to visit the house. However, he conferred on Ramji Sakpal a boon that a boy would be born in the family who would leave his mark on history. This boon took effect at Mhow on 14 April 1891. Mhow, the birth place of Dr. Ambedkar, is 630 km from Bombay by road via Nasik-Indore. It is 240 km from Bhopal, the capital of Madhya Pradesh.

Bhimrao, as the boy was named, was the fourteenth child of his parents. He was handsome and lovely. Perhaps, this led his kind-hearted mother, Bhimabai, to name him after her own name. Of the 14 children, only five survived—three sons and two daughters. Bhim being the youngest, the fourteenth jewel, was naturally the darling of the family.

Bhim was hardly two years old when his father retired in 1893 from the military service on a monthly pension of rupees fifty ;

came back from Mhow and settled down at Dapoli in the Konkan region of Maharashtra. Bhim's mother died in 1896. Same year, Bhim or Bhiva as he was also lovingly called, was sent to the primary school at Dapoli. Latter, his father got a job at Satara. There, Bhim completed his primary education and began his high school education at the Government High School. In the school records, his original surname was 'Ambavadekar' derived from his ancestral village 'Ambavade' as is the common practice in Maharashtra. This was, however, later changed to 'Ambedkar' by a kind high school teacher at Satara, whose own name was Ambedkar.

Being an untouchable by birth, Bhim faced and experienced as a child the same humiliations and difficulties which every untouchable had to face in those days. At school he was treated indifferently and insulted not unoften. Many a time he had to go without water, not because there was no water nearby but because he being an untouchable, had no right to drink from the common source. Bhim and his brother, Anandrao, were made to sit in a corner of the class on a piece of gunny bag which they carried to school. Some of the teachers would not touch their note books nor put questions to them for fear of being polluted. The Sanskrit teacher went a step further, and refused to teach Sanskrit to untouchables. As such. Bhim was forced to take Persian as the second language in the high school.

Similar was the attitude of the co-students of Bhim. He could not mix with them or play games with them. In illustration of the kind of treatment which Bhim received at the hands of his co-students, we might mention that one day when the teacher called upon Bhim to solve an arithmetical problem on the black board, there was uproar in the class and the caste-Hindu children cried out, saying that his touch would pollute their tiffins kept behind the board. Ultimately, Bhim was allowed to solve the problem only when the tiffin boxes were removed.

When the Satara assignment of Bhim's father was over, the family moved in 1904 to the cosmopolitan city of Bombay in a one-room tenament rented in the Improvement Trust Chawls at Parel. And Bhim joined the Elphinstone High School. Here too he was subjected to discrimination and suffered similar humiliations on account of untouchability. The treatment meted out to Bhim Rao outside school was even worse. "Touch me not" was the rule for him every where.

In 1907, Ambedkar passed his matriculation examination. This was considered such an extraordinary achievement by a Mahar boy that a public meeting was held by his kith and kin and other admirers to felicitate Ambedkar on his success in the examination. The meeting was presided over by S.K. Bole, a social reformer and leader of the Satyashodhak movement. One of the speakers at this meeting was Krishnaji Arjun Keluskar, a high school teacher, social worker, and scholar. He presented to young Ambedkar a copy of his recently published booklet in Marathi on the life of Gautama Buddha. This little gift awakened the mind of Ambedkar and he was so much fascinated by the life story of the Buddha that he resolved to make further study of Buddhism.

It is interesting to note how Keluskar, headmaster of the Wilson High School, first met Ambedkar in a city garden. Ambedkar used to go in the evenings to the Churni Road Garden in Bombay for study. Keluskar also frequented that garden for similar purpose. Charmed by the young studious student, Keluskar one day himself walked upto Ambedkar and enquired about him and his family. On knowing his background, Keluskar took a fancy for him and began helping him in studies.

After matriculation, Ambedkar joined the Elphinstone College. Keluskar took him to the Maharaja Sayajirao Gaekwad of Baroda, who had sometime earlier announced his intention to help the deserving students. The Maharaja asked Ambedkar some questions. Pleased with his answers, the Maharaja granted him a monthly stipend of twenty five rupees. Ambedkar graduated from the Bombay University in 1912. In January, 1913, he entered the service of Baroda State as a Lieutenant in the Baroda State Forces. He had, however. to return to Bombay just after fifteen days as his father fell seriously ill. The second day of February 1913 was the saddest day for Ambedkar as on that day his dearest father, who had sacrificed a lot for giving education to him, passed away. Now he was left to stand on his own feet. Once again, Keluskar who had since 1907 become a friend of the family, came to his rescue. On his initiative, Ambedkar was awarded a scholarship for higher studies in America by the Maharaja of Baroda. Accordingly in July 1913, Ambedkar joined Columbia University, New York, U.S.A.

Ambedkar worked very hard at Columbia keeping a study schedule of almost eighteen hours a day. He studied Economics, Sociology, History, Philosophy, Anthropolgy and Political Science. He was awarded the degree of Master of Arts on 2 June 1915 for his thesis 'Ancient Indian Commerce'. In May 1916, he presented a paper on 'The Castes in India : Their Mechanism, Genesis and Development' before the Anthropology Seminar organised at the University. In June, he was awarded the degree of Ph. D. for his thesis 'National Dividend for India : A Historical and Analytical Study' which was later published under the title ' The Evolution of Provincial Finance in British India". After completing his studies at Columbia University, Ambedkar came to London and joined the London School of Economics and Political Science for the degrees of M. Sc. (Economics) and D. Sc. (Economics). He also joined the Gray's Inn for law for the degree of Bar-at-Law. His admission into these prestigious institutions in London was greatly facilitated by the introductory letters given by his kind Columbia Professor R.A. Seligman.

Just after a year, when Ambedkar was hālf-way through, the Maharaja of Baroda, his benefactor, called him back as the duration of the scholarship granted to him was over. With a heavy heart, Ambedkar returned to India on 21 August 1917 without accomplishing his desired object. According to the bond, he was to serve the Baroda State for ten years. He was appointed Military Secretary to the Maharaja. The Maharaja's intention was to appoint Ambedkar his Finance Minister after some experience. But soon Ambedkar had to leave Baroda in sheer disgust in view of the continued harassment and ill treatment at the hands of the caste-ridden society. Even as a man of learning and high official in the State administration, he was subjected to inhuman treatment merely because he was born as an untouchable. Drinking water was not available to him in office. His subordinates kept distance from him. Even the peons, fearful of pollution, threw files and papers on to his desk from a distance. Recalling one such experience, Ambedkar later said, "As a man in the Accountant General's Office at Baroda, papers had to be flung at me instead of handed to me, and carpet had to be rolled back lest the highter castes stood on the same material as I stood on". At Baroda again, no one was willing to give accommodation to him. He somehow managed to hire a room in the local Parsi Dharmashala. But when the neighbours came to know about his identity, there was hue and cry and a mob of 15 to 20 armed men accosted Ambedkar and asked him to vacate the premises at once. As he could find no alternate accommodation of his own, he sent a note to the Maharaja, who directed him to the Dewan. As the Dewan also expressed his inability to do any thing in the matter, Ambedkar resigned and left Baroda in disgust. So he returned to Bombay in November 1917.

Such demonstrations of hatred and abhorence convinced Ambedkar that humiliation of his, and of his community, was because of the Hindu religion which had given birth to the curse of untouchability. He. therefore, took a solemn vow to try his utmost to free millions of his unfortunate brethren from the yoke of slavery.

On return to Bombay, Ambedkar spent about one year in wilderness, doing odd jobs. In the meanwhile, however, he got republished his paper on 'Castes in India', and also published a pamphlet titled 'Small Holdings in India and their Remedies'. In November 1918, he was appointed as Professor of Political Economy in the Sydenham College of Commerce and Economics, Bombay at a salary of of Rs 450 per month. Even here in the temple of learning, Ambedkar was treated as a pariah by the caste Hindu Professors and was not allowed to drink water from the pot kept in the professors' common room. He began organising his people in order to fight the injustice society. Carefully he surveyed the situation; reflected on the causes and came to the conclusion that their sufferings were multiplying as they had no voice, no resistance power, and no proper understanding of their slavery and serfdom. As a first step, therefore, he founded in January 1920, a Marathi fortnightly journal and named it 'Mook Nayak' (Leader of the Dumb). In the first issue of the spokesman in print of the dumbdriven masses, he laid emphasis on the awakening of the down-trodden from their age-old lethargy and in-action. He asserted that "in order to save the depressed classes from perpetual slavery, poverty and ignorance, herculean efforts must be made to awaken them to their disabilities."

An Ambedkar was keen to complete his unfinished studies. he saved some money for the purpose, got some help from the Maharaja of Kolhapur; resigned his post in March 1920 and proceeded to London to continue the studies of his own. In September 1920, he rejoined the London School of Economics and Political Science, and also the Gray's Inn for Law. Starting his studies afresh, he worked even harder than before. He joined all the important Libraries in London where he often pored over the books throughout the day without a break for lunch which he could also not afford. In June 1921, he was awarded the degree of M.Sc. (Economics) by the University of London for his thesis 'Provincial Decentralisation of Imperial Finance in British India'. In October 1922, he qualified for the degree of Bar-at-Law. About the same time, he submitted his thesis 'The Problem of the Rupee'. After submitting it, he went to Germany and joined the University of Bonn for further studies in Economics. He was there hardly for four months, when he was summoned to London by Professor Edwin Cannan as "the terse exposition in his thesis had given offence to the British imperialistic examiners who asked him to re-write thesis without changing his conclusions". This he did, and was awarded the degree of D.Sc. (Economics) by the University of London.

After successfully completing his studies in London, Ambedkar returned to India in April 1923. He was now thirty two. And having acquired the degrees of M.A., Ph.D., M.Sc., D.Sc., and Bar-at-Law from the Universities in America and England, he was the most qualified man in the country. To begin with, he started practice as a barrister in the High Court of Bombay. Here too he had hard times. "The solicitors would not condescend to have any business dealings with him on the ground of untouchability".

Dr. Ambedkar launched a concerted movement for the liberation of the untouchabes in July 1924 by founding the Bahishkrit Hitakarani Sabha (Association for the welfare of the Depressed Classes). The primary objects of this Sabha were to spread education, improve economic conditions and represent the grievances of the depressed classes. "Educate, Agitate and Organise" was the slogan of this Organisation. In order to reach the masses he started a Marathi weekly paper "Bahishkrit Bharat". He also founded in 1926 a militant organisation called Samta Sainik Dal or 'Social Equality Army'. First of all, he made the down-trodden people conscious of their miserable conditions and inspired them to struggle for their own betterment. This task he accomplished through his effective, inspiring and purposeful speeches and writings. He dinned into the ears of his people the mighty words of the Buddha: "Apply yourself to effort; strive for your own welfare; apply yourself to your own welfare; dwell heedful, ardent and resolute". And added, "we will attain elevation only if we learn self-help, regain our self-respect and gain self-knowledge". He often used to tell his people, "You must abolish your slavery yourself," and "It is disgraceful to live at the cost of one's self-respect". Never before such inspiring words worthy of instilling self-confidence in the dejected and distressed minds were heard by the suppressed masses Thus Ambedkar created a new awakening among them, and they responded to his call for action in a magnificent way.

The heroic struggle for the liberation of the untouchables from the yoke of social slavery was launched by Ambedkar on 19 March 1927 at Mahad, a picturesque town in the midst of hills and dales in district Kolaba of Maharashtra. Mahad is 175 km south of Bombay on the Bombay-Goa Highway. The Kolaba district has has since been renamed 'Raigad' to honour the memory of Chhatrapati Shivaji. The Raigad Fort, the Chief citadel of Shivaji, is only 25 km from Mahad.

In pursuance of a resolution passed by the Bombay Legislative Council in 1923, the progressive Mahad Municipality had thrown open the Chowdar Tank to the untouchables. However, the caste-Hindus were not allowing them to take water from the tank. The liberator and emancipator of the down-trodden, therefore, decided to launch an agitation to exercise the right of free access to the tank. In response to his call, about 10,000 men and men assembled at Mahad on 19 March. Next day, they began their march from the venue of the Conference to the Chowdar Tank to assert their right of nrinking water from the Municipal tank. Ambedkar was at the head of the procession. Ten thousand volunteers followed their leader in a file of fours. Wading through the street of Mahad in a disciplined and peaceful manner, the procession reached Chowdar Tank. Ambedkar, the most gifted and qualified untouchable ever born in India, asserted the right of the suffering humanity by drinking water from the forbidden tank. Most of the volunteers following him followed suit and vindicated their right. This was truly an historic event Never before the so-called Untouchables had demonstrated their determination to assert their right in such a glorious manner. The processionists then returned peacefully to the venue of the Conference. Meanwhile, rumour spread that Ambedkar and his men were planning to enter the temple of Veerashwar. The fanatic Hindus, who had failed to check the march of the untouchables to the Tank, swooped on the pandal. By that time, majority of the participants had left but a good uumber of them were still there, and were either packing or taking meals before dispersal. Thus the unarmed men, women and children were mercilessly beaten up by the caste Hindus. The commando attack on the pandal was followed up by attacks on splinter groups of the delegates returning to their villages. Inspite of all this beating and humiliation, Ambedkar advised his followers to be calm, and not to retaliate. Thus ended the first part of the epic struggle of the victims of untouchability.

Soon after news came that the orthodex Hindus had performed a tank-purification ceremony which they thought had been polluted by Ambedkar and his people. It is said that for purifying the tank, the Hindus took out water from the tank in 108 earthen pots. These pots were filled with curd, cow-dung, cow-urine and milk, and were dipped in the tank in the midst of chanting of mantras by the Brahmin priests. In the meanwhile, the Mahad Municipality also revoked on August 4, 1927 its resolution in accordance with which the Chowdar Tank was thrown open to the Untouchables.

This infuriated the Untouchables. It was a challenge to their self-respect and dignity as a community. Hence they dceided to besiege Mahad again, and assert their right, right of every human being, to take water from a public tank. Accordingly, a Satyagraha was planned for December 1927. Thousands of Satyagarahis reached Mahad on the evening of 25th December. Amidst tumultous scenes, the Conference, which, Ambedkar said, had been called to usher 'an era of equality', passed a number of resolutions aimed at the social, religious and political upliftment of down-trodden people. One of the resolutions related to Manusmriti, an old Hindu scripture which preaches inequality and directs the caste Hindus to award severest punishment if the Shudras dare to hear or read the Vedas. The condemnation of Manusmriti was not only confined to verbal resolution but a copy of it was also ceremoniously burnt in front of the pandal. This was done, as Ambedkar later explained because "the Untouchables view it (Manusmriti) as symbol of injustice under which they have been crushed across centuries."

The Satyagraha, planned to be launched on December 26, was in the ultimate abandoned following the pleadings of the District Collector who addressed the Conference and requested the delegates to await decision of the Court as some Hindus had filed a suit in the Court saying that 'the Tank is a private property. Before dispersing, however, the mammoth gathering went in a procession round the Tank, and then returned to the pandal. Thus ended the Mahad struggle. Verily, Mahad is a symbol of revolt. It is the Kranti Bhoomi.

The claim of the Untouchables to use the Chowdar Tank was finally accepted, after a long-drawn legal fight, by the Bombay High Court in 1937.

Finding in him an ardent champion of the cause of the depressed and suppressed, the Governor of Bombay nominated Ambedkar to the Bombay Legislative Council in 1927. Thus began the parliamentary career of the man who became two decades hence the chief architect of the Constitution of Free India. In 1928, Ambedkar was appointed Professor in the Government

Law College, Bombay. In February 1928, a Statuary Commission appointed by the British Government to re-examine and revise the Government of India Act, 1919 arrived in India. Ambedkar appeared before the Simon Commission on 23 October 1928 and demanded separate political rights for the Untouchables. The Report of Simon Commission was published in May 1930. As the Simon Commission was boycotted by some influential sections of people and its recommendations had no chance of being accepted, the British Government convened a tripartite Indian Round Table Conference to settle the framework of future constitutional set up for India. On behalf of the Depressed Classes, Dr. Ambedkar, alongwith Rao Bahadur Srinivasan, was invited to participate in this historic Conference, the first session of which opened in London on 12 November 1930. In his very first speech at this Conference, Ambedkar denounced all the sundry, including the British rulers for their indifference to the cause of the Depressed Classes, and demanded separate Political rights for the lowest of lowly in India. The first Round Table Conference continued its deliberations upto 19 January 1931. Ambedker played a significant role in all the sub-committees appointed by the Conference, and made his position amply clear so far as the rights of the Untouchables as a minority were concerned.

Impressed by the weighty arguments of Ambedkar, the Conference decided in principle to treat the Untouchables as a separate unit, and give them special representation in the future set-up of India. But the matter could not be finalised as the Congress had not participated in the first session of the R.T.C. Gandhi participated in the second session of the Round Table Conference as the sole representative of the Congress. In his very first speech on 15 September 1931, he opposed the special treatment for the Untouchables though he had no objection for special treatment to Muslims and Sikhs. However, all efforts of Gandhi failed. And inspite of his opposition, the British Prime Minister, Ramsay Macdonald, granted separate electorate to the Untouchables in the Communal Award published by him in August 1932. Having failed across the Table, Gandhi resorted to fast unto death in order to have the Award suitably amended. The Communal Award had, therefore, to be modified and replaced by the Poona Pact on 25 September 1932, which Ambedkar had to sign, in order to save the life of Gandhiji. Under the Poona Pact, separate electorate was replaced by joint electorate with 'reservation of seats' for the Depressed Classes. The concluding session of the Round Table Conference was held from 17 November to 24 December 1932, and as usual, Dr. Ambedkar participated in this session also. In the meanwhile, he was renominated for another five-year term to the Bombay Legislative Council.

Dr. Ambedkar's pilgrimage to Buddhism began unconsciously at Nasik. an ancient city on the banks of river Godavari. 184 km to the north-west of Bombay. It is said that it came to be known as 'Nasika' as here Sarupanakha's nose was cut off by Lakshmana. One of the oldest group of Buddhist Caves is at Nasik.

In this historic town of Nasik is the famous Kalaram Temple. This temple was chosen by Dr. Ambedkar to secure the right of entry into the Hindu Temples. The Satyagraha was planned for Sunday, March 2, 1930. The Satyagraha Committee which made arrangements for the satyagraha at Nasik was steered by Dadasaheb Bhaurao Gaikwad. In response to Ambedkar's call, about 15,000 volunteers assembled at Nasik.

On March 2, a mile long procession—the biggest procession in the history of Nasik, marched towards the temple. On reaching there, they found that the gates of the temple had been closed and there was heavy police bando-bast. The processionists, therefore, proceeded to the Godavari Ghat and held a meeting there.

The Satyagraha began on march 3, by way of small groups going to the temple and courting arrest. The Satyagraha continued for more than a month. When on April 9, the day of the chariot procession of the image of Rama, some satyagrahis attempted to reach the chariot, as had been agreed to by the trustees of the temple, some caste Hindus lost their senses and ambushed the unarmed untouchables with stones and lathis. A large number of them, including Ambedkar, were injured. Inspite of all this, the struggle was carried on, and the trustees of the temple had to keep the temple closed for a whole year. The Nasik satyagraha continued for over five years and then it was called off as the lesson had been drawn 'No More Hindu Temples'.

As the Temple Entry Satyagraha at Nasik failed to bend the caste Hindus Dr. Ambedkar summoned a conference at the nearby town of Yeola, on 13 October 1935 to decide the future course of action. Addressing the mammoth gathering, he recounted the plight of the Untouchables in all spheres, and the sacrifices made by them 'to secure the barest human rights as members of the same community under the aegis of Hinduism. He went on to say that the time had come to decide if it was not better for them to abjure Hinduism and embrace some other faith that would give them an equal status, a secure position and rightful treatment.' Speaking about himself, Ambedkar said 'Unfortunately, I was born a Hindu. It was beyond my power to prevent that, but I solemnly assure you that I will not die a Hindu"

After careful consideration, the Conference resolved to abjure Hinduism, and to stop the Nasik satyagraha as the past five years had demonstrated the futility of such agitation against the caste Hindus, who had thwarted all their attempts to regain honourable status.

Thus ended the Yeola Conference with a message of 'Good-bye to Hindu Religion'. And a search for New Religion began.

When Dr. Ambedkar announced his intention to discard Hindu religion, there were tempting offers by the Christians, Muslims and Sikhs to attract him towards their religions. But he scoffed at these offers, and rejected the same without hesitation. On learning of the Yeola announcement, Venerable Lokanatha, an Italian Buddhist monk, came to India toward the end of 1935 and met Dr. Ambedkar several times at his residence, Rajagraha, in Dadar, Bombay and impressed upon him that Buddhism was the most suitable religion for his followers. Dr. Ambedkar promised to consider.

The year 1935 is significant for three other happenings in the life of Dr. Ambedkar. He lost his loving wife, Ramabai, on 27 May 1935. Four days later, on 1st June, he was appointed to the post of Principal of the Government Law College which position he held for three years till he resigned in 1938. In 1935 again, he built his house (residence-cum-library) at Dadar, Bombay and named it

'Rajagraha' after the capital of Bimbisara of Magadha, where the Buddha had often sojourned.

In December 1935, Dr. Ambedkar was invited by the Jat-Pat-Todak Mandal of Lahore to preside over their Annual Conference to be held in the last week of March 1936. He accepted the invitation and took pains to prepare his Presidential address in which as was expected, he not only condemned the caste-system and the Hindu religion in the harshest language but also went on to add that 'it was the last speech he was going to deliver as a Hindu'. The Mandal asked him to delete these words and other objectionable portions from the address. As, however, he refused to do so, the Mandal Reception Committee cancelled the Conference. Ambedkar did the next best thing. He published his undelivered address in the form of a pamphlet and "the posthumous child of the Conference has survived the passage of time as a great thesis on the annihilation of caste."

In order to explain the reasons as to why he had decided to change his religion, Dr. Ambedkar convened a Mahar Conference in Bombay on 30 and 31 May 1936. Concluding his forceful speech at this Conference, he said: "The Hindu religion does not appeal to my conscience. It does not appeal to my self-respect. However, your conversion will be for material as well as spiritual gains. I tell you very specifically, RELIGION IS FOR MAN AND NOT MAN FOR RELIGION. To get human treatment, convert yourselves".

Finally, he exhorted the vast audience to remember the last words of the Buddha to Ananda, "Be ye lamps unto yourselves. Betake yourselves to no external refuge. Hold fast to the Truth as a lamp. Hold fast as a refuge to the Truth. Look not for refuge to anyone besides yourselves." This gave an indication the way his mind was working.

"Hunger is the greatest disease", so said the Buddha. Realizing that the Untouchables not only suffered from 'hunger' but also suffered from numerous social disabilities, Ambedkar consciously decided to go slow with his plans for conversion to another religion. Instead, he directed all his energies towards the social, economic and political emancipation of his followers. And to achieve his objective, he made consistent efforts and resorted to all ways and means at his disposal.

In purusance of the decisions taken at the Round Table Conference, the country went to the polls in February 1937 to elect India's first popular legislatures. The Independent Labour Party founded by Ambedkar in August 1936 bagged 15 seats, out of 17 seats it contested in Bombay. As a leader of opposition, Ambedkar played a very effective and purposeful role in the Bombay Legislative Assembly and endeavoured to ameliorate the condition of the down trodden people through legislative measures. The Provincial Assemblies came to an abrupt end in November 1939 in eight provinces, including Bombay, when the Congress Ministries resigned as a protest against the British Government's failure to declare their war aims and their policy towards India's freedom.

In August 1940, the British Government declared its policy of grant of Dominion Status to India as soon as possible after the war. In July 1942, the Viceroy of India expanded his Executive Council and included Dr. Ambedkar as Labour Member in it. This was the glorious moment. He had risen from dust to doyen. His elevation to the highest position ventilated recognition of his sterling qualities of head and heart. His appointment as Labour Member was welcomed by all in view of his keen interest in the welfare of labour ever since his entry into the public life. As Labour Member from July 1942 to June 1946, Ambedkar trackled a number of knotty problems of labour to the satisfaction of the employees and the employers alike. He also introduced a host of labour welfare measures. All this won him esteem and respect from all concerned, and he was hailed, even by his critics, as an able and benevolent administrator. For the Scheduled Castes, he secured for the first time the principle of 'reservation' in the Government services ; thus opening for them the outlet for their social and economic uplift.

After the cessation of hostilities of the second world war in 1945, the question of India's freedom assumed priority. In March 1946, the British Government sent a three-man Cabinet Mission to study the situation in India, and to suggest the ways and means for the smooth transfer of power to Indian hands. On 16 May 1946, the Cabinet Mission announced their proposals recommending inter-alia the setting up of a Constituent Assembly to frame a Constitution for the future governance of India. The Cabinet Mission Plan was accepted by all concerned. Then followed elections to the Constituent Assembly ; Members being elected by the Provincial Legislative Assemblies on the basis of population. Dr. Ambedkar's efforts to get elected from Bombay were thwarted by the Congress, but he managed to enter the Constituent Assembly through the Bengal Assembly.

Having regard to his ideological differences with the Congress Party which dominated the Constituent Assembly Dr. Ambedkar could expect nothing more than placing his view point before the Assembly. However, as soon as the Assembly met, not only his presence was welcomed, his co-operation and assistance was also solicited by some prominent Congress members in framing the Constitution. On his part, Ambedkar too reciprocated the gesture. In his maiden speech in the Assembly on 17 December 1946, he forcefully pleaded that, notwithstanding their differences, the various parties and groups "should take a decision in common and march on the way which leads to unity". This set the process of reconciliation into motion. Later, the "very useful" work done by him in various sub-committees of the Constituent Assembly convinced the Congress leaders beyond doubt that without Ambedkar's services, the legislation and solidification of freedom would not be easy. No wonder, the Congress Party which had opposed tooth and nail his entry into the Constituent Assembly a few months earlier, came forward to sponsor his candidature when Ambedkar lost his seat consequent upon the division of Bengal.

Accordingly. Dr. Ambedkar was re-elected from Bombay in July 1947 as a member of the Constituent Assembly. Soon thereafter, Prime Minister Jawaharlal Nehru invited him to join his Cabinet to be formed on the eve of Independence on 15 August 1947. Considering it in larger interests of the country, Ambedkar agreed to join the Cabinet. Thus he had reached the pinnacle of glory at the dawn of Independence. Immediately after his appointment as Minister of Law, the Nation bestowed upon Dr. Ambedkar another honour. On 29 August, the Constituent Assembly unanimously elected him as Chairman of the Drafting Committee which was assigned the task of giving final shape to the Constitution. The Constitution of the Republic of India is, therefore, largely the creation of the master mind of Dr. Ambedkar.

After marathon sessions for about three years, the Constituent Assembly successfully accomplished the task assigned to it in November 1949. The Assembly began the third reading of the Constitution Bill on 17 November 1949. Dr Ambedkar replied to the debate in the afternoon of November 25. Speaking with a feeling of great relief, he highlighted the salient features of the Constitution and thanked the Assembly for having given him an opportunity of serving the country. The Assembly adopted the Constitution on 26 November 1949.

As the Chief Architect of the Constitution, Dr. Ambedkar was largely responsible for incorporating the safeguards for the Scheduled Castes and Scheduled Tribes in the Constitution. He also became intrumental in legally abolishing the curse of untouchability. He was responsible to a great extent for the adoption of the Buddhist symbols : Dharmachakra (the Wheel of Law) and Lion-Capital of the Asokan Pillar at Sarnath as National symbols of free India.

Dr. Ambedkar was also keen to ameliorate the condition of women. In order to confer on them equality in the matter of property, marital relations and adoption etc., he drafted and introduced the Hindu Code Bill in the Constituent Assembly (Legislative) on 24 February 1949. As the ideas of Ambedkar to unify the Hindu Code were progressive and in tune with the modern thought, handsome tributes were paid to him by many progressive leaders. But his efforts to codify and liberalise the Hindu Law were virtually wrecked by the protagonisits of orthodoxy. Disappointed and dejected, therefore, he resigned from the Nehru Cabinet on 27 September 1951. Six months later, he was elected to the Council of States, the Rajya Sabha.

On 5 June 1952, Columbia University in America from where he had taken his first Ph. D., thirty-six years earlier in 1916, conferred on Ambedkar the degree of LL.D. (honoris causa) hailing him "as a framer of India's Constitution", and "One of India's leading citizens, a great social reformer and a valiant upholder of human rights". Later, the Osmania University, Hyderabad, conferred on Dr. Ambedkar an honorary degree of D. Litt.

While busy in state affairs, Dr Ambedkar also kept on thinking of ways and means to emancipate the down-trodden masses of India. In 1942, he founded the Scheduled Castes Federation, and began organising the Scheduled Castes on all India basis. His preference for Buddhism became vocal in 1945. In November of that year, a Provincial Conference was held at Ahmedabad on the banks of Sabramati and its spacious pandal was called 'Buddhanagar'. In 1945, the founded the People's Education Society, and in June next year he established the first college at Bombay and named it 'Siddharath College'. Symbols as these clearly indicated the trend of his mind and were a writing on the wall for his followers So they sought advice from him as to how best to understand and follow the marvellous Dhamma. In response to their persistent requests, Dr. Ambedkar got reprinted in 1948 Prof P.L. Narasu's book 'The Essence of Buddhism' first published in 1907, and recommended it for study to the would be Buddhists. In the preface to this book, he also mentioned that he was himself writing a book on Buddhism.

He also delved into the past of the Untouchables, and published his findings in 1948 in his book, 'The Untouchables-Who were They and Why They became Untouchables'. According to him, the present day Scheduled Castes were Buddhists in distant past and were condemned as Untouchables in about 400 AD during the reign of the Gupta Kings. Some other important books published during this period were : Who were the Shudras ? How they came to be the Fourth Varna in the Indo-Aryan Society; What Congress and Gandhi have done to the Untouchables ; and Pakistan or the Partition of India.

In the midst of all this, Dr. Ambedkar married, on health grounds, Dr. Miss Sharda Kabir on 15 April 1948.

In 1950, it became perfectly clear that embracing of Buddhism by Dr. Ambedkar was a matter of time only. In that year, he asked his followers to celebrate the Buddha Jayanti. In the celebrations in Delhi he himself participated. Thus on 3 May 1950, Delhi witnessed a Buddhist procession for the first time some thousand years after the disappearance of Buddhism from India. Same year, he contributed an article for the first time in the Vaisakha number of the Maha Bodhi journal of Calcutta under the title 'Buddha and the Future of His Religion'. Summing up his thoughts on Buddhism, he said in this article that he preferred Buddhism because he found the religion of the Buddha rational, scientific, and an epitome of liberty, equality and fraternity.

On 25 May 1950, Dr. Ambedkar reached Colombo for participating in the First Conference of the World Fellowship of Buddhists, and same day he attended the inaugural session of the Conference which was held at the Temple of the Tooth in Kandy. While in Sri Lanka, he also addressed the Young Men's Buddhist Association on the "Rise and Fall of Buddhism in India". Concluding his speech, he said, "Buddhism may have disappeared in material from but as a spiritual force it still exists in India". On return from Sri Lanka, wherever he went, Dr. Ambedkar talked about Buddhism, its past glory and its future prospects. At a meeting held on 29 September 1950 at the Japanese Buddhist Temple in Worli, Bombay, he declared that he would devote the rest of his life to the revival and spread of Buddhism in India. In 1950 again, he visited the famous Sanchi Stupa. Vincent Shean, an American who accompanied him on this trip, records : "On one occasion we journeyed together on a train to Sanchi and back to Delhi-a long journey-and spent our day at the Buddhist shrine down there, the great stupa where the relics of the disciples now lie. Even then (1950) Ambedkar knew a great deal about Buddhism and lectured me upon it at inexhaustable length".

In 1951, Dr. Ambedkar participated in the Buddha Jayanti celebrations organised by the Maha Bodhi Society of India, New Delhi. Speaking on this occasion, he declared : "If the rest of the Hindu Society does not co-operate, then we, the members of the Scheduled Castes, will go on our own and try once again to bring back Buddhism to its former glory and prestige in this country". Same year, he also published, for the benefit and guidance of his followers, 'Baudh Upasana Path'—a collection of Buddhist Suttas, which are gems of wisdom, And in the April-May 1951 issue of the Maha Bodhi, Ambedkar contributed a scholarly article "The Rise and Fall of the Hindu Woman. Who was responsible for it". In this article he conclusively showed that the Buddha had endeavoured to ennable woman and raise her to the level of man. Same year in July he founded the Indian Buddhist Society to work for the propagation of Buddhism.

When Dr. Ambedkar established the first college in Bombay, he named it as 'Siddharath College' after the personal name of the Buddha. But he could do no more than giving it a Buddhistic name since ready-made buildings were purchased for this purpose. He was, however, keen to establish an institution through which the glory of Buddhist art and culture could be perpetuated. For this experiment, he chose Aurangabad, an ancient seat of Buddhism, in the heart of the backward region of Marathwada. The college at Aurangabad was named the Milind Maha Vidyalaya, after the Greek King Minlinda or Menander who carved out a kingdom in Punjab in second century B.C., and later embraced Buddhism. In the Buddhist lore, the names of Milinda and Bhikkhu Nagasena always go together. Dr Ambedkar too honoured both the philosopher king and his preceptor. The vast campus of the Milind Maha Vidyalaya has been made as Nagasena-Vana. The foundation stone of the Milind Maha Vidyalaya was laid by Dr. Rajendra Prasad, the President of India, on Ist September 1951.

By 1954, it had become abundantly clear that embracing of Buddhism by Dr. Ambedkar was only a matter of time. He was often seen in the company of the Buddhist monks and scholars. In May 1954, he spent two weeks in Burma attending the Buddha Jayanti celebrations there. In June, he anounced his intention of starting a Buddhist seminary at Bangalore to train preachers for the propagation of Buddhism in India. Speaking in the series 'My personal Philosophy' in a BBC broadcast on 3 October 1954, he said : "My social philosophy may be said to be enshrined in three words : liberty, equality and fraternity. My philosophy has roots in religion and not in political science. I have derived them from the teachings of my Master, the Buddha".

In the first week of December 1954, Dr. Ambedkar again visited Burma to participate in the Third Conference of the World Fellowship of Buddhists held at Rangoon. Addressing the Conference, he said, "I have to say this with great anguish that in the land where the Great Buddha was born, His religion has declined. How such a thing happened is beyond any one's comprehension." After saying this, tears came into his eyes and he could not proceed with his speech for a few moments. Later, he gave a brief resume of his plans to revive Buddhism in India and emphasized that gigantic amounts being spent on the lighting and management of the shrines could be usefully used for the propagation of the Dhamma and its revival in India.

While in Burma, Dr. Ambedkar visited Mandalay, where he stayed for a week as guest of Dr. R. L. Soni, a Punjabi who had gone to Burma in 1929; settled there; embraced Buddhism and was working hard for its revival through the world Institute of Buddhist Culture founded by him. The historic decision to come foremally to Buddhism in 1956 was taken by Dr Ambedkar at Mandalay. There was lot of discussion with Dr. Soni on the merits of coming formally to Buddhism. Ultimately on the 5th day of his stay there, he announced: "It will delight you to know that I have finally decided to come formally to Buddhism alongwith my followers in the 2500th year of the Buddha, i. e. in 1956 of the common calendar". And, he added: "In this interval I will be able to solve some problems to facilitate the way".

On return from Burma, the first thing Dr. Ambedkar did was to reform and register in June 1955 the Buddhist Society of India. And on 25 December 1955, he installed the Buddha image, presented to him in Rangoon, in a newly built Vihara by his followers at Dehu Road, near Poona, Addressing the gethering on this occasion, he indicated his plans to embrace Buddhism within a year.

In May 1956, Ambedkar gave a talk over the BBC, London on "Why I like Buddhism and how useful it is to the world, in its present circumstances". In the same month he sent his monumental work 'The Buddha and His Dhamma' to the Press. And on

24 May 1956, the 2500th Buddha Jayanti Day, at a public meeting held at Nare Park, Bombay, he announced that he would embrace Buddhism in October. Thereafter, he thoughtfully selected the date for this historic event, and requested the Most Venerable Maha Thera U Chandramani of Kushinagar to lead him to the blessed religion of the Buddha at Nagpur on 14 October 1956, the Vijaya Dashmi day. This day was chosen as it was the auspicious day of Dhamma-Vijaya, the day on which Asoka the Great had embraced Buddhism in B.C. 262 and had declared that henceforth he would conquer the people by love and persuation instead of by force. Giving reasons as to why he had selcted the city of Nagpur for the Great Conversion Ceremony, Dr. Ambedkar said: "Those who have studied the Buddhist history of India know that the people who worked in the beginning for the propagation of the religion of Buddha were the 'Nagas'. It was the Nagas who spread the religion of the Buddha throughout the world. These people were predominently the inhabitants of Nagpur. Through the soil of this city there flowed a river named the 'Nag'. It appears that the Nagas lived on the banks of this river. This is mainly the reason for selecting Nagpur for this great occasion".

For this historic ceremony, a fourteen-acre vacant Plot of Government land near the Vaccine Institute at Shardhanand Peth was selected as venue. At the northern end of the huge pandal stood a huge rostrum which tastefully decorated with buntings and with the five-hued Buddhist flags, stood a huge rostrum lined with white cloth and surmounted by a replica of the Sanchi Stupa.

On the bright morning of Sunday, 14 October 1956, lakhs of people men and women, who had been pouring into the Nagpur city by train and bus from all parts of Maharashtra or had trekked on foot hundreds of miles, prepared themselves for the ceremony wearing white ctothes. Procession after procession of white-clad men and women with Buddhist flags in their hands made their way to the Deeksha Bhoomi or the Initiation Ground. By 9 AM they had reached the site and turnd into a vast ocean of humanity.

When Babasaheb Ambedkar, accompanied by his wife, and N. C. Rattu, his private secretary, reached the pandal, the vast crowd lustily cheered their uncrowned king. Wearing the white silk dhoti and white coat, he was seated at the dias next to Venerable U Chandramani Maha Thera, the eldest and seniormost Buddhist monk in India. Seated in the second row were Devapriya Valisinha General Secretary of the Maha Bodhi Society of India, Venerable monks, and some leading members of the Buddhist Society of India founded by Babasaheb. About four lakhs people witnessed the auspicious ceremony which began at 9.40 A.M. The 80 year old Ven. U Chandramani of Kushinagar administered in Pali to Dr. Ambedkar and his wife, the Tisarana (Triple-Refuge). Standing solemnly before the shining image of Lord Buddha, they recited three times "Buddham saranam gacchami, Dhammam saranam gacchami, Sangham saranam gacchami." The three Refuges were followed by the Five Precepts (Panca-Sila). They repeated the same in Marathi. Then they vowed thrice with clasped hands before the Buddha image and offered white lotus flowers before it. With this, the conversion ceremony was over. When Dr. Ambedkar's entry into Buddhism was announced, the vast concourse of humanity gathered there gave thu derous applause and raised full-throated cries of Victory to Lord Buddha' 'Victory to Babasaheb Ambedkar'. Thereafter, Dr. Ambedkar was profusely garlanded by D. Valisinha and other dignitaries present there.

The historic Nagpur ceremony marked the end of pilgrim's journey. Addressing the vast gathering, Dr. Ambedkar, now a Buddhist, said in an emotional voice : "I started the movement of renouncing the Hindu religion in 1935 and since then I have been continuious struggle. This conversion has given me enormous satisfaction and pleasure unimaginable. I feel as if I have been liberated from hell.'

He then called upon those to stand up who were prepared to em brace Buddhism. Thereupon, the entire crowd rose as one man. And in loud and joyous tones they repeated the Three Refuges and the Five Precepts after Babasaheb In addition, he alse administered to them the twenty-two vows which he had specially prepared to ensure that his followers renounce their old religion fully and become good Buddhists.

Of these special vows, the first eight vows require the initiate into Buddhism not to worship the Hindu gods and goddesses; not to regard the Buddha as an incarnation of Vishnu; not to perform the traditional Hindu rites for the dead; and not to employ Brahmin priests for any rites and ceremonies. The next two vows lay equality of all human beings. The vows from 11 to 18 emphasis on call upon the new initiates into Buddhism to practioe the Noble Eightfold Path and the Ten Paramitas and to lead a life in which Knowledge, Right Conduct and Compassion are harmoniously interwoven. The last four vows practically sum up all the vows. These vows enjoin upon the new comer to renounce Hinduism because it is based on inequality and adopt Buddhism as his religion; to firmly believe that the Dhamma of the Buddha is the true religion; to believe that he is experiencing a (spiritual) rebirth; and to solemnly declare and affirm that hereafter he will lead his life according to the teachings of the Buddha.

On the next day, the vast crowd again assembled at the same place to hear the roaring voice of their liberator. Before he spoke, another conversion ceremony was held to admit into the fold of Buddhism about one lakh men and women who had arrived late the previous day and could not participate in the initiation ceremony. Thereafter, in his three hour long speech, Dr. Ambedkar traced the history of the sufferings of the down-trodden people through the ages; his life-long struggle to mitigate therir sufferings; and as to why he had chosen Buddhism of all the religions. Spelling out the reasons for this change, Dr.. Ambedkar said, "Man cannot live by bread alone. He has a mind which needs food for thought. Religion instils hope in Man and drives him to activity' Hindu religion has watered down the enthusiasm of the down-trodden. That is why I found it necessary to change my faith and embrace Buddhism." Continuing he said that "the Hindu Society was based on Chaturvarna which is another name for inequality. In this religion there is nothing but slavery and serfdom for the depressed and oppressed-classes. In remaining in its fold it will not do any good to us. Our salvation lies only in religion of the Buddha which is based on equality and universal brotherhood."

After the great event was over, Dr. Ambedkar felt greatly relieved. He gave vent to his feelings in his letter dated 30 October 1956, to Devapriya Valisinha, General Secretary of the Maha Bodhi Society of India, Calcutta: In this letter, which is almost like a Last Will, he wrote :

"Thank you very much for your letter of 25th October 1956. It certainly was a great event and the crowd that came forward for conversion was beyond my expectation. Thank the Buddha it all went well.

I am glad you realize that having begun the task well we have to look its continued progress in the future. We have to consider ways and means of imparting knowledge of Buddhism to the masses who have accepted His Dhamma and will accept it on my word. We should no doubt train a large number of workers to teach the Dhamma to the people, but the best agents for carrying out the same are the Bhikkhus. They would carry a great deal of prestige with them which no layman could do.

The Bhikkhus in my judgement ought to be very happy to find out that a large task awaiting them has been done. The only difficulty with the Bhikkhus is that they don't care to learn the language of the people. I am afraid the Sangha will have to modify its outlook and instead of becoming recluses they should become like the Christian missionaries social workers and social preachers. As I told you, today they are neither Arhans nor useful members of the Society. This fact must be hammered into them and make them realize that they could serve the Buddha well by becoming preachers of His Dhamma.

I like your idea of opening a sort of a logical seminar where Bhikkhus and non-Bhikkhus could be taught the fundamentals of Buddhism and made to learn the different languages of India so that they could be sent to the different parts.

The conversion ceremony in Bombay will probably take place in December, most probably during the Xmas holidays, so that many people could have travel facilities which they would not otherwise get. I shall let you have the exact date after consulting my Bombay people.

I hope you are giving full publicity to the Nagpur ceremony in the Maha Bodhi Journal. I would like you to particularly mention the following points :

1. That on the first day some three lakhs and eighty thousand people became converts to Buddhism. As many people arrived after the ceremony was over and a second ceremony was held on the next day as the first item in the programme.

2. That there was another conference at Chanda on 16th October 1956 which was held in the evening. There also another conversion ceremony was held and some 3 lakhs of people were converted.

3. That I am receiving letters from all corners for conversion.

With reference to your querry as to our tour programme, I am told a copy of the same has already been sent to you. You will know from it when I shall be in Sarnath."

Four weeks after the historic mass conversion ceremony at Nagpur, Dr. Ambedkar visited Nepal to participate in the Fourth World Fellowship of Buddhists Conference held in Kathmandu from 15--21 November 1956. This was his first appearance as a formal Buddhist at an international gathering. He received tremendous ovation at the Conference. Describing the Nagpur event as a 'miracle' Dr. G.P. Malalasekera, President of the W.F.B., said in the inaugural session on 15th November: "We are living in an age of miracles of many sorts. We see them happen around us frequently. I will refer only to one of them by way of example. Till a few years ago, Buddhism had almost disappeared from the land of its Founder. But, in the recent past, it has been making its presence felt as a presage of things to come. Just one month ago, on the 14th October, to be precise, we saw a miracle happen when at Nagpur 500,000 people, embraced Buddhism under the leadership of Sri B.R. Ambedkar. Never before in the history of any religion in the world had half a million people declare themselves the adherents of a new Faith on a single occasion. It was a stupendous event and already its far reaching effects are becoming manifest. It has set in motion a series of chain-reactions. News come daily from far and wide from many parts of this subcontinent of large masses of men and women following this heartening lead. Events such as these fill us with joy and hope."

Thrilled by the Nagpur miracle, the world Buddhist community was eager to hear the views of Dr. Ambedkar on the present day problems facing Buddhism, particularly the challenge of Communism. Responding to their request, he addressed the

Conference on 20th November 1956. Concluding his thought-provoking hour-long speech, he said : "Do not be allured by Communist successes. I am quite confident that if we all become one-tenth as enlightened as the Buddha was, we can bring about the same result by the methods of love, of justice and goodwill".

Though sick yet on his way back from Nepal. Dr. Ambedkar went on pilgrimage to the holy Buddhist shrines. On 23 November, he worshipped at the Great Maha Bodhi Temple. From Bodh Gaya, he came same evening by train to Sarnath where he stayed for three days at the newly built Rest House. On 25 November, he addressed about 150 monks from various Buddhist countries and urged them to take up the Dhamma-duta work more seriously in India ; visited the Sarnath ruins, the Dhamek Stupa and worshipped at the Mulagandhakuti Vihara. He also addressed a series of meetings at Sarnath-Varanasi. On 27 November, he left by air for Gorakhpur on his way to Kushinagar. After worshipping at the sacred Parinirvana Temple of Buddha, he returned to Delhi on 29 November. Next day, he presided over a meeting of the Scheduled Castes Federation at which it was decided to shed the communal approach to politics and march along with the other toiling masses on the basis of equality. The S.C.F. was accordingly disbanded and a new political party open to all was formed. The formation of the Republican Party of India turned out be his last act

Five days later, on the evening of 5 December, he asked for the Preface and Introduction to 'The Buddha and His Dhamma' to be given to him, so that he could work on them during the night. But this was not to be. He passed away in sleep in the early hours of Thursday morning, 6 December 1956. All over the world the news of his sudden demise was received with surprise and shock. The Nation deeply mourned the unexpected demise of Dr. Ambedkar. His followers were especially non-plussed. They simply did not know what to do. They felt orphaned. After careful consideration, the body was taken to Bombay by his stunned followers and cremated there, according to Buddhist rites, on 7 December 1956. More than 500,000 people joined the funeral procession, the biggest such procession ever seen in the city of Bombay, and it took nearly four hours to cover a two mile distance from Rajgraha, his residence, in Dadar to the local burning ghat, near Shivaji Park. Babasaheb had planned a mass conversion ceremony in Bombay on 16 December. To fulfill his wish, about 100,000 people insisted that they be admitted into the fold of Buddhism. Hence, an impromptu conversion ceremony was organised at the cremation ground, and they were administered the Three Refuges and Five Precepts on the spot by Bhadant Anand Kausalyayan.

Such was the charisma of Dr. Ambedkar. He was a great man. His death proved greater than his life. His message "to follow the Buddha" was well-taken by his people

EPILOGUE

The Buddhist revival movement began in 1891 with the founding of the Maha Bodhi Society by Anagarika Dharmapala, a young Sinhala Buddhist, who turned out to be the first great Buddhist missionary of modern times. By 1956, the Maha Bodhi Society and other pioneers were able to create a lot of awareness about the rich heritage of Buddhism but they were not able to attract many adherents to its fold. In 1891, India had 50,000 Buddhists and, after sixty years, in 1951, the Buddhist population in India had risen only to 1,80,823. Even out of this figure, over 90% were the traditional Buddhists living in the high Himalayan valleys where Buddhism had survived through the ages. Thus till then, the impact of the revival movement was not much.

Then came Dr. B. R. Ambedkar, the modern Bodhisattva, who performed a miracle at Nagpur on 14 October 1956 by bringing about five lakh people to the fold of Buddhism. In fact, it was a great miracle. Never before in the history of any religion in the world, so many people. at one time and at the instance of one man had changed their religion. Unfortunately, Dr. Ambedkar suddenly passed away on 6 December 1956. This was the blackest day for Buddhism in India. And the most unfortunate part of it was that it came so soon after the brightest day, 14 October. Just seven weeks earlier, Dr. Ambedkar had given a clarion call to his followers to seek refuge in the Buddha-Dhamma. They had not yet even understood the relevance of the new parth shown to them by their liberator and emancipator. And he was no more. Inspite of this tragedy, the conversions continued unabated. No wonder, the 1961 Census revealed a still greater miracle. The Buddhist population in 1961 showed an unprecedented increase of 1671%, that is, from 1,80,823 it rose to 32,50,227 just in five years (1956-61). In the case of Maharashtra the home state of Babasaheb Ambedkar, the increase was the maximum; from a meagre figure of 2, 487 in 1951, the Buddhist population there rose to 27,89,501 in 1961. In 1981, the population of Buddhists in India was 47,19,796 constituting 0.71% of the total population of the country.

The Buddhists of modern India can be divided into four distinctive groups. Firstly, there are survivals from the Buddhist period. Secondly, there are ethnic over-laps from the neighbouring countries. The third category is represented by those who were attracted toward Buddhism as a result of the missionary movement spear-headed by the Maha Bodhi Society. The followers of Dr. Ambedkar form the fourth group. Of all the groups, the followers of Dr. Ambedkar form the most dominant group. They are over 90% of the total Buddhist population in India. Of them, about 84% live in Maharashtra alone. Thus the credit for making Buddhism once again a living religion in India goes to Dr. Ambedkar. Verily, he was the Greatest Pioneer

SOURCES

General

Maha Bodhi Society of India Diamond Jubilee Souvenir–4-A Bankim Chatterjee Street, Calcutta, 1952.

2500 Years of Buddhism, ed P.V. Bapat, Publications Division, Government of India, Delhi, 1956.

Buddhism in Modern India, D.C. Ahir, Nagpur, 1972.

The Indian Discovery of Buddhism–1855—1956, Eleanor Zelliot, Studies in Pali and Buddhism, A Memorial Volume in honour of Bhikkhu Jagdish Kashyap, ed. A.K. Narain, B.R. Publishing Corporation, Delhi, 1979.

Baudh Vibhutian (Great Buddhists) in Hindi, Bhikshu Dharmarakshita, Sarnath.

Individual

1. Flame in Darkness–The Life and Sayings of Anagarika Dharmapala, Maha Sthavira Sangharakashita, Triratana Grantha Mala, Pune, 1980.

– Article 'This Journal' by St. Nihal Singh, The Maha Bodhi 2500th Buddha Jayanti Vaisakha Number, Volume 64, May 1956.

– The Diary Leaves of the late Ven Anagarika Dharmapala, February and March 1899, edited by D. Valisinha, The Maha Bodhi, Volume 71, March-April 1963.

– The Diary Leaves of the late Ven. Anagarika Dharmapala, April 1899, edited by D. Valisinha, The Maha Bodhi, Volume 71, September 1963.

– The Diary Leaves of the late Ven. Anagarika Dharmapala, May, 1899, edited by D. Valisinha, The Maha Bodhi, Volume 72, February 1964.

2. Devapriya Valisinha, A Biographical Sketch by Gee Tsing Po, Calcutta, 1962.

– Sri Devapriya Valisinha Memorial Number, The Maha Bodhi Volume 76, August-September 1968.

3. The Maha Bodhi, Volume 76, November-December 1968 (Ven. K. Sriniwasa).

4. The Maha Bodhi, Volume 74, November-December 1966 (Ven. D. Sasanasiri).

5. The Maha Bodhi, Volume 91, October-December 1983 (Ven. N. Jinaratana).

6. The Maha Bodhi, Volume 93, July-September 1985 (Ven. U. Dhammaratana).

7. The Maha Bodhi, Volume 93, January-March 1985 (Ven. M. Sangharatana).

8. Bhikshu Chandramani Mahasthavir Ka Jeevan Parichay (Hindi) by Bhikshu Gyaneshwar, Kushinagar.

9. My Non Violence, An Autobiography of a Japanese Buddhist, Nichidatsu Fujii, translated from Japanese by T. Yamaotri, Japan Buddha Sangha Press, Tokyo, 1975.

10. Baudh Vibhutian (Hindi) by Bhikshu Dharmarakshita, Sarnath.

11. Hemendu B. Chowdhary, Bengal Buddhist Association and its President Kripasaran Mahathera, Bengal Buddhist Association, I Buddhist Temple Street, Calcutta, 1987.

12. Dharmananda Kosambi (Marsthi) by Dr. P.V. Bapat, Souvenir, Bahujana Vihara Buddha Jayanti Celebration Committee, Parel, Bombay, 1969.

13. Bhadant Bodhanand Sthavir (Hindi) by Chandrika Prasad Jagiasu, Bahujana Kalyan Parkashan, Lucknow, 1965.

14. Prabhakar Machwe, Rahul Sankrityayan, Sahitya Akademi, New Delhi, 1978.

— Bhadant Anand Kausalyayan, Rahul Sankrityayan (Hindi), People's Publishing House, New Delhi.

— Mahapandit Rahul Sankrityayan's tribute to Bhadant Bodhanand Mahasthavir published in the biography of Bhadant Bodhanand (Hindi) by Chandrika Prasad Jagiasu, Lucknow, 1965.

— Selected Essays of Rahul Sankrityayan (On Way to Tibet), People's Publishing House, New Delhi, 1984.

15. Smarnika (Hindi) published on the occasion of the 80th Birthday of Bhadant Anand Kausalyayan, Buddha Bhoomi, Khairi Road, Kamptee, Nagpur, 1985.

16 Studies in Pali and Buddhism—A Memorial Volume in honour of Bhikkhu Jagdish Kashyap, A K. Narain, Delhi, 1979.

17. All Assam Buddhist Association, Desangpani, sub-division Dibrugarh, Assam (Ven. Nandabansa).

18. Bhikshu Dharm Rakshit (A Life Sketch), Udai Narain Pande, Kushinagar Bhikkhu Sangha, Kushinagar.

— Baudh Dharm hi Manav Dharm, Dr. B.R. Ambedkar, compiled and edited by Bhikshu Dharmarakshita, Mamta Prakashan, Varanasi, 1967.

19. The Life and the Work of Ven. L. Ariyawansa Maha Thera, Srinivas Pathak, Maha Bodhi Society of India, Mandir Marg, New Delhi, 1980.

— Buddhism in the Capital of India, D.C. Ahir, New Delhi, 1969.

20. Ladakh Buddha Vihara, Bela Road, Delhi (Ven. Kushak Bakula).

21. South India Buddhist Association, Perambur, Madras (Pandit Ayodhya Dasa).

22 Preface by Dr. B.R. Ambedkar to the Third Edition of The Essence of Buddhism by P. Lakshmi Narasu, Delhi, 1948.

22. M.B. Society Diamond Jubilee Souvenir, 1952—C. Krishnan.

24. Ibid.—Dr. Anandrao L. Nair.

25. Ibid.—Pandit Sheo Narain.

26. Hemendu B. Chowdhary, Calcutta.

27. The Maha Bodhi, Volume 70, June 1962—N.K. Bhagwat.

28. The Maha Bodhi, Volume 90, January-March 1982—The Chogyal of Sikkim.

29. Dr. Soni Number, The Maha Bodhi, Volume 83, January-March, 1975.

30. Dr. Ambedkar. Life & Mission, Dhananjay Keer, Bombay, 1954.

— Buddhism and Ambedkar, D.C. Ahir, New Delhi, 1968.

— Gandhi and Ambedkar, D.C. Ahir, New Delhi, 1969.

— Dr. Ambedkar and Indian Constitution, D.C. Ahir, Lucknow, 1973.

— Dr. Ambedkar on Buddhism, D.C. Ahir, Siddharth College, Bombay, 1982

— Dr. Ambedkar's written speech in Marathi at the Mahar Conference held in Bombay on May 30-31, 1936. It was first published in the special issue of 'Lok Rajya' published by the Government of Maharashtra on 16 April, 1981.

— The Maha Bodhi journal, Calcutta, Volume 84, November 1956 (Dr. Ambedkar's letter dated 30.10.1956 to Devapriya Valisinha).

— Report of the Fourth Conference of the World Fellowship of Buddhists held at Kathmandu, Nepal, in November 1956, published by the Dharmodaya Sabha, Kathmandu, Nepal, 1956.

Appendix

FRIENDS OF BUDDHISM

When Anagarika Dharmapala, a young Sinhala Buddhist, arrived in Calcutta in 1891, he was alone, a stranger in an alien land, fearing that he might be lost in the metropolitan city of Calcutta. His amiable nature and devotion to the Buddha, the greatest son of India, however, stirred the conscience of the Bengali elite, bhadralok, and many of them came forward to help him in his noble task of reviving the ancient glory of Buddhism in India, the land of its birth. Of these, the four most prominent ones were : Narendra Nath Sen, Editor of the 'Indian Mirror' who helped Dharmapala in various ways ; Neel Comal Mookerjee, a businessman, whose home became Dharmapala's home in his earlier years in Calcutta as he extended hospitility both freely and cordially ; Sir Ashutosh Mookerjee, a Judge of the High Court and Vice-Chancellor of the Calcutta University, who was elected President of the Maha Bodhi Society in 1916, and continued to hold that office till his death in 1924 ; and Manmatha Nath Mookerjee who was President of the Society from 1925 to 1942. Dr. Shyama Prasad Mookerjee was the last Hindu to head the Maha Bodhi Society of India from 1942—52.

Among those who came to regard Buddhism "as a high point of Indian Civilization", mention may be made of : Sir Hari Singh Gaur who was the Vice-Chancellor of the Nagpur University and a member of the Central Legislative Assembly. He published his famous book 'The Spirit of Buddhism' in 1928 ; Kashi Prasad Jayaswal whose home in Patna served as a centre for the preservation of the large material on Buddhism brought by Rahul Sankrityayan from Tibet ; and Har Dayal, the well-known revolutionary and freedom fighter of Punjab. In 1911, he went to Harvard University in America to study Buddhism but soon left the University and joined the Indian revolutionaries there. From the freedom struggle, he once again came back to the studies and joined in 1927 the School of Oriental and African Studies in

London. Here, as his Ph.D. thesis, he produced his book 'The Bodhisattva Doctrine in Sanskrit Literature' which still remains a standard work in this field. Har Dayal considered Buddhism as the only answer for the eradication of evils like caste-system from the Indian society.

Two eminent poets—one British and the other Indian—who worshipped the Buddha and made Him popular through their poetry were : Sir Edwin Arnold and Gurudev Rabindranath Tagore.

Sir Edwin Arnold (1832-1904), the world famous poet and author of The Light of Asia was born in Great Britain. He landed in India in November 1857, at the age of 25, on his appointment as Principal of Deccan College, Poona. Enchanted by the Indian religious lore, he was soon attracted by Buddhism. Though Arnold returned to London in 1861 to take up an assignment with the 'The Daily Telegraph', his interest in Buddhism continued to grow, and flowered in the shape of an epic poem, The Light of Asia. First published in 1879, this beautifully written biography in verse of the Buddha achieved instant success and popularity in the West. In India too, it became the most popular book to be studied in schools and colleges, and attracted many persons to Buddhism.

The national poet, Gurudev Rabindranath Tagore (1861 1941), not only made the Buddha "the subject of moving and colourful lyrics, ballads, plays and dance-dramas, but also poured out his warmest admiration and worship to the words, achievements and personality of the Buddha declaring Him the greatest man in the whole world history".

Unlike the people of the Calcutta, the people of Benaras (Varanasi) showed complete indifference towards the Buddhist cause. Anagarika Dharmapala was keen to make Sarnath, the site of Buddha's First Sermon, a living shrine once again. Hence, he constructed there a beautiful temple, the Mulagandhakuti Vihara, towards the fag end of his life. The citizens of Benaras did not contribute even a single penny towards the cost of this Vihara. Sri Prakasa, who later became Governor of Assam, Madras and Bombay successively, and was Treasurer of the Mulagandhakuti Vihara Building Fund says : "We cannot be sufficiently grateful to the great Anagarika Dharmapala who, despite all the difficulties that be-set his path, has established the Mulagandhakuti Vihara at the famous Deer Park. To me it is a matter of shame that Benaras which it embelishes and which is the home of so many creeds and faiths, and which has been made sacred by its association with some of the greatest men and women of the world, including the Great Buddha Himself, should have been indifferent to the memory of the Lord and should not have contributed anything to the building of the temple which tells the world where Buddha preached His first sermon-the place where He turned the Wheel of Law-made the Dharma-Chakra Pravartana". (The Maha Bodhi, Vol. 46, October 1938, pp. 433-34).

What has been said about the attitude of the people of Benaras is generally true of other parts of North India as well. However, with the opening of the Mulagandhakuti Vihara at Sarnath in 1931, things began to change, and some enlightened Hindus came forward to help the revival movement. One of them was Seth Jugal Kishore Birla (1881-1967), the well-known industrial magnate and a great philanthropist of Pilani, Rajasthan. In 1934, he built a magnificent Dharmashala at Sarnath for the convenience of the pilgrims visiting holy Isipatana. Similarly, he built two other Dharmashalas at Bodh Gaya and Kushinagar. He also constructed the beautiful Buddha Vihara at New Delhi (1939) for the Maha Bodhi Society. He also made a donation of Rs. 25,000 towards the construction of the Maha Bodhi Welfare Home at Calcutta. Besides all this, he also helped the Maha Bodhi Society in various other ways. Birlaji also financed the construction of the Bahujana Vihara at Parel in Bombay founded by Dharmananda Kosambi in 1937 as well as the Japanese Buddhist Temple at Worli, Bombay built in 1940.

One of the greatest friends of Buddhism in modern India was Jawaharlal Nehru (1889—1964), the first Prime Minister of India. Born at Allahabad, he was drawn to Buddhism quite early. He says : "The Buddha story attracted me even in early boyhood, and I was drawn to the young Siddhartha who, after many inner struggle and pain and torment, was to develop into the Buddha. Edwin Arnold's 'Light of Asia' became one of my favourite books.

In later years when I travelled about a great deal in my province, I liked to visit the many places connected with the Buddha legend, sometimes making a detour for the purpose". (Discovery of India, p. 120).

Nehru's association with the Buddhist movement began in 1931 when, along with Sri Prakasa who was then Treasurer of Mulagandhakuti Vihara Building Fund, he attended the inaugural function of the Mulagandhakuti Vihara at Sarnath in November 1931. Although he did not speak at the gathering, he announced that he would send a replica of the then national flag as momento to the Vihara. This promise was faithfully kept and some time later a silver replica of the Congress flag encased in a sandalwood box was sent to the Vihara, In the following years, Jawaharlal Nehru participated in two anniversaries of the Mulagandhakuti Vihara ; besides visiting Sarnath of and on.

The first important event in the Independent India which focussed the attention of the Indian masses on the virtues of the Buddha-Dhamma was the return and restoration of the sacred relics of the two chief disciples of the Buddha, namely, Sariputta and Maha Moggallana at their original resting place at Sanchi. The sacred relics of the two saints landed on the Indian soil, after about a century of their journey to London in 1851, on 13 January 1949 and were welcomed with due honours on board H.M.I.S. Tir by Dr. Kailash Nath Katju, Governor of West Bengal. Jawaharlal Nehru, the Prime Minister of India, himself went down to Calcutta and received them at the Raj Bhavan. He also presided over the mammoth public meeting held in the Calcutta Maidan on 14 January 1949 to accord them a reception. Later on, he instructed the Government to give all facilities for the safe-keeping of the relics and for their transport to several States in India and also to some countries abroad. When the relics reached New Delhi on their way to Ladakh in Kashmir, Nehru came to the New Delhi Buddha Vihara, on Mandir Marg, to pay his respects, and on their return from Ladakh he again came to the Vihara with his daughter Mrs Indira Gandhi to bid them farewell.

The celebrations of the home-coming of the relics of Sariputta and Moggallana were concluded with a grand function at Sanchi, near Bhopal, in November 1952. The Prime Ministers of India (Nehru) and Burma (U Nu), Dr. S. Radhakrishnan, the Vice-President of India, World Buddhist leaders and many Venerable Bhikkhus attended this function. Speaking on this occasion, the Prime Minister, Jawaharlal Nehru, said that he saw in the teachings of the Buddha a path leading to progress and prosperity and that he had made it his life mission to make other people conscious of this revelation to him. He further said that the incident of the homecoming of the relics had deeper significance to his mind and that the significance would be realised when all of them had made a living temple in their hearts enshrining ancient memories for guidance in this confused world. Concluding Nehru said : "Out of this Conference a seed will bloom and spread happiness".

The most important and abiding work that Nehru did for Buddhism was on the occassion of the 2500th Buddha Jayanti Celebrations in 1956. While laying the foundation stone of the Memorial Monument (Buddha Jayanti Park) on the New Delhi Ridge on 23 May 1956, Jawaharlal Nehru said: "the 2500th Buddha Jayanti Celebrations mark the home-coming of the Buddha". It was largely because of his deep respect and reverence for the Buddha that to celebrate the historic Buddha Jayanti in a befitting manner, the Government of India appointed a Celebrations Committee headed by Dr. S. Radhakrishnan Vice-President of India. Other members of this Committee were : Dr. Sampurnanand, Chief Minister of U.P.; Dr. Sri Krishna Sinha, Chief Minister of Bihar; S.D. Sharma; Chief Minister of Assam; Ven. Kushak Bakula of Ladakh and the Maharaj Kumar of Sikkim. As a result, the Government organised the year-long celebrations and spent over a crore of rupees in restoring, repairing, and renovating the Buddhist shrines.

The last act of the benevolent Prime Minister Nehru was the opening of the Ladakh Buddha Vihara on Bela Road, Delhi, on 24 February 1963. The Rest House attached to the Vihara was constructed by the Government at a cost of Rs. 5 lakhs for the use of Buddhist pilgrims from Ladakh and other border areas in response to a request made by Ven Kushak Bakula to the Prime Minister of India.

Jawaharlal Nehru passed away on 27 May 1964.

Index

(a) Persons

(b) Places